Journey to
A True
Self

Copyright © 1999, 2007, Curtis Wall

All rights reserved. Printed in the U.S.A.

No part of this publication may be reproduced or transmitted in any form or by any means, electronic or mechanical, including photocopy, recording or any information storage and retrieval system now known or to be invented, without permission in writing from the publisher, except by a reviewer who wishes to quote brief passages in connection with a review written for inclusion in a magazine, newspaper or broadcast.

Published in the United States by
Beckham Publications Group, Inc.
P.O. Box 4066, Silver Spring, MD 20914

Library of Congress Control Number: 2007924320

ISBN: 0931761719

978-0-931761-72-0

Journey to a True Self

Growing From Moments of Pain

Curtis D. Wall

Beckham
PUBLICATIONS GROUP, INC.
Silver Spring

My name is Curtis D. Wall:
The D stands for Daring, Dashing, Debonair, Dynamic.
I am a tremendously Fascinating Human Being.
I'm not the Best, but I'm in the Top Two.
I'm not always Right, but I am never Wrong.
Damn, I'm Good.

(By the Grace of God)

This book is dedicated (in memory) to my brother Paul.

Paul died at the age of 36 in an officially recorded automobile accident. There is little doubt though in my mind that Paul committed suicide. I believe that he lived in this world for 35 years and never knew what it felt like to truly love himself, nor actually feel the love of another human being. Neither one of us was shown much love during those all important formative young years. Consequently, we both had a tremendous battle trying to come to the point of acquiring love of ourselves and, thereby, expressing love to those around us. Both of us experienced tremendous verbal, mental, emotional, and physical abuse at the hands of our father. And both of us grew up believing that "nobody" really cared about us. The pain, agony, doubt, rejection, and lack of self-love that permeated our lives proved, in his case, insurmountable. Yet, according to those relatives and acquaintances who acknowledged having some awareness about our emotional plights, "Paul would likely be the one to survive, to make it." Of course, that turned out not to be the case.

To Paul: I know that you have finally found that peace of soul that you were never able to find while "existing" in this world. I Love You.

Acknowledgments

I gratefully thank the following for their encouragement, motivation, and indulgence throughout this project: my wife, Evelyn; my children, Chloe and Curtis, Jr.; A.E.S., K.T., M.M. (inspirators) and R.N., Ph.D., for her spiritual uplifting at a time in my life when I needed it most; Ms. Ruth Hickman of the College-East Campus, Polkton, North Carolina, for her painstaking efforts in editing this writing; to Dr. Randy McPherson of Memphis, Tennessee for his diligence in proofreading also, and finally, to my Higher Power, whom I choose to call God, without whose omnipresent Grace, none of this would be possible.

Introduction

Psychologists and developmental experts have long advocated that the basic human personality is formed, for better or worse during the initial six or seven years of one's life. There are obvious and powerful influences on the human psyche. Among those influences are home and environmental tenets, the absence or presence of love, security and nurturing. We become what we experience. If the experiences during those times are more positive than the negative, we tend to grow into some semblance of the normal human being. We are able to consistently go about the business of mastering our potential, inner strength and power. The contrary has proved to be true if there exists a greater and more profound degree of negativism during that period of time. The gamut stretches from moderately under- and over-developed states of emotional security to true clinical mental illness.

During those formative and trying times, at a conscious level, we are all but defenseless against whatever onslaught that may come our way. Some of us will retreat within ourselves, while others of us seek that much harder to impress the significant other(s). Confusion and mixed emotions generally abound. The subconscious self does all it can to shield and protect us from the abuse. Defense mechanisms roar into action, allowing us to maintain as best we can. The resilient nature that is inherent in all of us begins to exert itself as well. The level and extent of that exertion is directly proportionate to the amount of downlifting (vs. uplifting) that we receive.

The road to achieving a sufficient measure of wholeness and self-acceptance will more than likely be difficult traveling. In order to fully make use of our innate talents and gifts, though, we must choose to make that journey. The central thing that is essential to any of us reaching that plateau of destiny is the will to overcome, the will to rise above the pain and mental and emotional anguish. In spite of our negative state of being when caught up in the throes of that darkness, we must want with all our heart and soul to discover our path to recovery. Only then will the mechanism to change be granted to us. That ability to change the negative state to a positive one becomes a reality. At that point there is no way for it not to occur. And, of course, we receive the necessary help from selected human beings along the way. Though core aspects of this healing process are the same for all of us, the specific directives surrounding it tend to be as unique as we are individual. It is truly a journey to true self...

    I believe this book is divine in its conception and execution and that it will find its way into the hands of people who can benefit from it. Everyone has a story; this is a part of mine and my struggle to find and accept who I am. I believe there will be many who will identify with the thoughts, feelings, situations and experiences. I believe there will be those of you who will be inspired to overcome your own personal pains, tragedies and disappointments. I hope to encourage you not to give up on yourself and your pre-ordained destiny. I want to encourage you to steadfastly travel whatever path that you must travel to reach that point of forgiving, accepting and loving yourself, stretching inward and upward toward fulfillment of your purpose for being on this planet. This is my prayer. I thank you for choosing to spend some of your time with me.

Contents

Dedication 6
Acknowledgments 7
Introduction 8

1. The Birth of the Marred Psyche 13
2. Impacts 33
3. (No) Sex, Drugs and the Blues 48
4. Uncle Sam (Doesn't) Want Me 68
5. A Geographical Cure 87
6. The Miracle 109
7. Letting Go and Moving On 116
8. Living Human, Living As Myself 128
    Fear
    Therapy
    Anger
    Dreams
    Running
    Mind Games
    Holidays
    Psychosomaticism
    The Addictive Personality
    Spirituality vs. Religion
    Family
    Friends and Friendship
    Race
    Teenagers
    The Martyrdom Complex
    Authority Figures
    Music
9. The Reconnected Psyche: A Final Look 155

1
The Birth of the Marred Psyche

"...With each successive blow from the seemingly endless barrage of the 2 x 4, the pain grew more intense. Finally, I would feel the pain no more as darkness corralled my mind, and I lost consciousness..."

I have replayed that scene in my mind a thousand times over. A great deal of time would pass before the intensity of that Moment would begin to wane. That incident would turn out to be one of many unpleasant experiences that would shape me as a person, shape my view of you, and shape my view of my purpose for being on this earth.

***

A midwife delivered me in the late afternoon of November 24, 1954 in a large wooden frame house. The house was complete with *all sides air conditioned,* as the air pockets between the boards were numerous and wide in various places. Large window fans would otherwise complete the task of cooling us during the summer months. I was described by relatives as being a pretty baby during those infant times. Years later, that perception was to change dramatically. I would apparently lose that once angelic glow and innocence. It would be turned in and exchanged for an internalized view of physical unattractiveness to include a near constant facial expression of combined pain, anger, fear and sadness.

The extended family concept was definitely in effect in our

house at that time – being populated with grandparents, aunts, uncles, brothers, sisters, cousins, and, of course, my Mom, Ruth. Mom had returned to Morven, North Carolina to give birth to me. This appears to have been a pattern. Mom would live and work in Camden, New Jersey, with my father, Vick; get pregnant, and then return home shortly before the baby was due. Mom, Paul, and I would rejoin Vick several months later in New Jersey.

That five-room house in Morven, North Carolina, had a tin roof that leaked off and on in various places during rainy weather. There were two beds in every room except the kitchen, excluding the guest room which contained only one bed. We lived rent free because everybody who was old enough to work made themselves available to the landlord on a year-round basis. We were basically sharecroppers. Mr. Ratliff, a white man, was one of the area's major cotton producers. Everybody that I knew referred to him as Mister Ratliff. He was a pleasant enough man who would always speak. At the same time, an air of superiority was a constant. During the early days I remember the house had open fireplaces in two of the rooms, a wood-burning heater in the guest room, and a wood-burning stove in the kitchen. We would later upgrade to wood-burning heaters in all the rooms, and eventually replace one of those with a coal-burning heater. The day the coal-burner arrived, I remember thinking how uptown we had become.

The house had no running water or inside plumbing. We got water from a pump that was in the back yard approximately 20 yards from the kitchen porch. Every night about dusk, two water buckets would be filled and brought into the house for overnight usage. Baths were taken in the same tin washtub, that our clothes would be washed in once a week. At one point we ironed our clothes using a non-electric iron that we heated up via the open fireplace. The venerable outhouse where bathroom privileges were exercised was situated about 150 yards from the house. At night time we would bring in the white ceramic pot, or the piss pot as Mister Ratliff referred to it, that was about a foot and a half deep – for urination purposes. We called it simply the night pot. The nearby field, which was closer than the outhouse, oftentimes served as the more preferable location for exercising the other bodily function.

My family would not vacate that house for one with inside plumbing until 1976. Another family would move in almost immediately, this house being considered a step up for them. While we were there, the tin had to be replaced every three or four years. The tin would be a shiny metallic sort that especially stood out from a distance. The kids we rode the bus to school with would snicker among themselves for a week or two after the new tin had been put on. I was embarrassed and I think my brothers were also. I took the laughter personally, allowing it to feed into my always poor image of myself. The laughter at our house that came from the young girls seemed to bother me more so than the guys' laughter.

We raised a lot of our own food. We had one cow for milk and butter and a horse named "Tom" for plowing and pulling the flat bed wagon. We would occasionally mount Tom's back for a brief jaunt in the pasture area near the barn. I fell off the horse one day during my early attempts to ride him. While the tears came, I recall being put back onto Tom almost immediately by someone. Riding the wagon being pulled by Tom one lazy afternoon down a dirt road continues to be a vivid and fond image.

The men folk would hunt rabbits and squirrels for additional meats; the younger folk would fish, (bull) frog and turtle hunt. I learned the art of skinning and cleaning the rabbits and squirrels from watching the older males. Hogs and chickens were our primary sources of meat. In fact, killing a hog was a semi- major event in that country hood I was growing up in at that time. The hog meat we would eat-on year round. We would breed, feed, kill and cure (dry and salt) the meat, storing most of it in the smoke house that sat about 15 yards diagonal to the back porch. I detested having to feed the pigs morning and evening. The smell of the slop definitely turned me off to the entire process. The pigs usually met their demise by a 12 gauge shotgun blast or an axe blade to the center of the forehead. Very little, if any of it, ever went to waste. It was a tradition to share some of the meat with family, friends and neighbors.

The hog brains served as a morning delicacy for mostly the

old folks. The brains were oftentimes mixed with an egg. I remember trying the dish once and not being very impressed. I think I had more difficulty getting past the "hog brain" distasteful image in my mind than anything else. Fatback, from the hog also, was cooked nearly every morning as well. To eat fatback was considered by us younger folks to be a definite clue of being poor. You can imagine how my brother and I must have felt being forced to carry fatback biscuit sandwiches to school for lunch. We would often consume the biscuit prior to getting on the school bus or simply toss it after reaching the designated bus stop area. We would oftentimes suffer through the lesser humiliation of not having anything to eat at lunch rather than deal with the teasing brought on by actually being seen eating a fatback sandwich. At no time do I recall any kid admitting to consuming fatback, even though I knew there were several of them worse off financially than my family was.

On special occasions, usually when the preacher came for Sunday dinner or out of town relatives visited, we would chase down one of the chickens, grab the head and neck and wring it off in one quick motion. I remember being fascinated watching the chicken's body continue to jump spastically for a few Moments after its body hit the ground. They tended to be much tastier that those we bought from the store. Still, at least five chickens would be purchased from the grocery store on a weekly basis. We had to purchase very few eggs as the hens in the barnyard were bred primarily for egg production. Paul would refuse to eat chicken, raised or bought, claiming an allergy to them (until he became an adult). I have oftentimes wondered if his watching one of those withering chickens – in pain and confusion – early on had somehow played psychological havoc with him in some way – that in combination with his own physical and emotional abuse.

Uncle *TC* generally was the one who milked the cow each morning, though I drew that duty a couple of times, in his presence of course. I had to have been around five or six years old at that time. Churning the milk into butter seemed to be a task that befell me more often than I wanted it to. I ate a great deal of cornbread and buttermilk during those times, almost on a daily basis. I consumed so much then, that I have more than a slight problem with both cornbread and buttermilk today. I just got worn out on them. Back then I ate it out of necessity because of the scarcity of the snack food supply, but I actually liked the combination in the beginning. It was like one of those always available in-between meal snacks.

Everybody basically worked in the fields, picking cotton for $2.50 - $3.00 per hundred pounds and chopping cotton for three dollars per day. We younger males would pull weeds for 75 cents per 4-6 hours a day. We also would pick boll weevils from cotton for one cent each, along with any odd jobs that came along. We would commence duty with the field tasks around 6:00 a.m. and conclude near dusk. Rarely were new clothes purchased for us, other than our one pair of shoes per year. More often than not they were bought used, sometimes too small, sometimes too big. Hand-me-downs were our reality for the most part. We were taught, however, to be grateful for what we had, which was difficult for me a lot of the time. The truth of the matter was, there were other people, other kids in the area, as with the fatback, that actually had it much worse than we did. Most folks would pretend to have more that what they really had.

****

My first official memory in life is apparently not a legitimate memory at all. In fact, according to confirmed reports, it would have to be an impossible one. I have pictured, me as a small child finding Grandpa Moses lying unconscious next to a small stream in a wooded area near our house. I remember he was stretched-out on his back with a most peaceful look about his face. I thought it was explained to me not long afterwards that Grandpa Moses had an apparent heart attack that day down by the stream and one of my adult relatives and I were the ones to discover him.

My grandfather actually died in 1947, seven years before I was born. I would have to have been told of the circumstances surrounding my grandfather's death and somehow to have mentally affixed the death scenario as described above. Right?

A huge canvas picture of him hung in the den. Even when direct questions were asked, the most popular response was generally, "He was a good man," regardless of what the specific question might have been.

My second official memory in life is me again as a small boy; around the age of four. The image of me standing and looking out the den window in a white T-shirt and turned-up blue jeans is still vividly clear. I recall asking myself while standing there peering out at what seemed like a tremendous volume of cars and trucks in our backyard: "Why are all these people at our house?" That scene turned out to be a wake for my mother who had just died. She was 33 years old. There is a vague picture in my mind also of one of the female adults gathering un children into a room and telling us, "Ruth's dead." I honestly do not recall my specific reaction to the news. I am sure it was a normal one of sadness, disbelief, and abandonment. The abandonment theme would hand around for almost a lifetime with me. As we will talk about later, much healing had to occur around the issue of "Mom leaving me."

To this day, I do not consciously recall what my Mom looked like. There are no photographs of her or of us as a family. The one picture I do recall seeing had been taken outside, with the sun casting a glare over Mom's face, making it unrecognizable. Even that photo has long since disappeared. I have been told that

I favor her, as opposed to my father. Throughout the years, I have heard basically the same things about my Mom said repeatedly by the people who knew her: "She was a good person, but she was a bit of a rebel." In fact, the old folks used to say that her dying at such a relatively young age was God's way of punishing Mom for her rebellious ways, which had, perhaps, included the occasional use of alcohol and her taking little flack from anyone - other than my father.

Shortly after my birth, Mom, Paul and I, did, indeed, join father in Camden. It was there that Mom became pregnant again, this time with my younger brother

Emmanuel. I have no recall of this period of time in my life. I have been told by older relatives that all three of us (Mom, Paul and myself) were routinely physically, emotionally and mentally abused by "daddy-dearest". It was relayed to me (at age 39) that I was the victim of sexual abuse as well, of which I have no recollection. After numerous threats from Grandma Wincy and Co., my father eventually dropped all of us back off in Morven shortly before Emmanuel's birth.

Per the already established pattern, the drop-off would have probably occurred anyway, without the threats.

I would be 39 years old before I was emotionally forced to search out the truth about Mom's death. She died February 6, 1959, from hypertension complications the day after giving birth to my youngest brother, Emmanuel. Per the talk again, my father was in New Jersey at the time of her death "shacking up" with another woman. Yes, some of the anger still lingers. Mom had consciously made the choice not to abort the baby; she had been warned by her doctor that severe health complications would likely result during the birth procedure. The issue of poor pre-natal care was present also; as word has it, my father refused to take Mom to a physician on any type of routine basis. It was common for the women folk back in those days not to drive or even have a driver's license. I assume that Mom had to rely on my father (or some other male) to take her places not within walking distance. Without expressed permission, no other man would dare transport another man's wife anywhere. I can visualize Mom "sucking it up" and hoping things would turn out okay in spite of the lack of appropriate medical care. In addition, Mom had chronic high blood pressure and a diabetic condition.

****

A feeling of dread still occasionally rises in me when I think about my father returning (actually, he sent Mrs. May and her husband – his duplex neighbors in New Jersey) - to pick up Paul and me two years later, following Mom's death. I will never forget the words that came from Mrs. May's mouth as she stepped out of the "55 Studebaker, "Vick wants his boys," meaning Paul and me.

It is unclear if Larry and Emmanuel were a part of that request. Aunt Marie immediately said no to Larry (her favorite) being taken; and she refused to back down. Larry had been born 14 months prior to Emmanuel. His birth had been complicated as well, most likely due to Mom's increasingly deteriorating physical health and the lack of proper pre-natal care. Larry would be born a "blue baby" (lack of sufficient oxygen). He would live with a fear of dying prematurely for 21 years. He did not share those thoughts and feelings with me until after he had beaten the odds. At the time of his revelation, I remember his voice filling with anger more than anything else. Babies born in such a condition generally died prior to the age of 21, so said the old folks.

Emmanuel had already been taken of by Mom's brother after her death. This was a done deal also. Realizing what was happening and coming to the understanding that no one was going to fight to keep Paul and me, I made a beeline to and underneath the crawl space of our house, banging my head as I scampered away from Mrs. May on my hands and knees, while crying and screaming at the same time. "No, I don't want to go back!" would come out of my mouth over and over again. I can see myself bug-eyed and weeping traveling underneath the crawl space at near lightning speed in my attempt to escape. My heart pounded with ever increasing rapidity as I made it a little more than midway toward the rear of the house. I could not go any further in that direction without getting down on my stomach. I simply stopped, sat up on my behind, placed my head down on top of the back of my hands and bawled. When I was eventually coaxed from underneath the house I was still wailing. The tears would finally stop after several more minutes. I had accepted my lot.

Even though Grandma hated allowing this to happen, she felt she did not have a choice. They couldn't keep all of Vick's kids from him. Additionally, my father had instructed Mrs. May to tell Grandma that he was going to treat us better this time. The knifing feelings of, "Nobody loves me; nobody wants me," vibrated throughout my entire being. Somehow, because Larry and Emmanuel were saved by other family members, this edition of "Life with father in New Jersey," I internalized to mean that they were loved, but Paul and I were not. I felt betrayed. Fear gripped me with a stranglehold. Even though I could not consciously remember at that particular Moment why I dreaded so badly going back to live with my father, I just knew that I did not want to! Paul and I would both lose out. We were packed up and taken back to Camden that same evening.

The only part of the journey back to Camden that I can remember is our going through the New Jersey Turnpike, and my wondering if the water above us would come crashing down on us before we reached the other side. Looking back I can now see the analogy – of the water overhead and me in the "tunnel" – experiencing fear and distrust of man's physical construction; having fear and distrust of man's ability and inclination to de-construct (destroy) a human soul. I sat motionless, nearly paralyzed, that evening for that stretch of our journey in the back of the '55 Studebaker. Paul's demeanor was nearly identical to mine. The little boys, the already lost children, were headed back to hell. At the ages of six and seven, we would be nearly helpless, not able to protect ourselves, either physically, mentally or emotionally. But somehow we had to survive; somehow, we would survive.

***

Vividly, clear in my mind still is the sight of Paul climbing up on top of a woodpile our first evening back with our father and sitting down and commencing to cry – for what seemed like hours. That scene became an almost daily ritual for Paul, always around dusk. He would cry and I would stand below the woodpile and watch him, with me hurting like hell at the same time. I would not allow my tears to come though. Sometimes my chest would swell with painful emotions to the point where I felt as if it was going to explode. Still, I would not let the tears come. I was well on my way to becoming the "Iceman," a nickname I would pick up during my undergraduate college days, so said because of my penchant for rarely displaying outward emotion.

On our second or third day back, Paul and I were introduced to the woman whom our father was involved with – at that time. She would ask me to come over and give her a kiss on the cheek. I refused. My father would join in with the encouraging of me to kiss the lady: "Come on boy," he would say. Though I feared my father, I still refused to move toward her. The lady would then offer me a dime for a peck on the cheek; my father would simultaneously advise me in a much stronger tone of voice to do what the lady was requesting. This time I did.

It seems like it took me forever to walk the few feet across the floor to her and kiss her on the cheek. I thought about Mom as I made the journey. And I was filled with much sadness… and anger. The dime meant nothing in terms of motivation to comply; it was the change in my father's tone of voice that spurred me into the desired action. The reasons for dreading returning to him was becoming clearer with each passing Moment. I have no recollection of seeing the woman again after that day, even though I am sure she continued to come around.

Sometimes I wonder if my subconscious, in an effort to protect me from the pain of Mom not being there with me, blocked further memories of this lady from my mind.

We would eat a basically apple and rice diet over the next one and a half year period; the apples would come from four trees in the back of the complex. I don't recall who actually cooked the rice, but it showed up nearly every day along with the apples. In hindsight, such a diet was nutritional, but it was the lack of serious effort on the part of our father to provide more of a variety that was hurtful. It would appear that the food had to be either cheap or free. He was not so financially strapped that he could not have done better. During the summer months when school was out, Paul and I would work alongside the grown-ups eight to ten hours a day cutting asparagus, and picking tomatoes and cucumbers.

Even after school would resume, we were expected to help out if the vegetable fields were within walking distance of the complex. I am sure that those work experiences contributed greatly to my lifelong attitude of having no problem engaging in difficult labor. When we were not in the fields, Paul and I basically supervised ourselves. There was no baby-sitter. I'm sure that at the ages of six and seven we were expected to fend for ourselves and we did.

Both Paul's and my school records were supposedly lost when sent from Morven, North Carolina to Camden, and I strongly believe that they probably were not ever requested. Instead of being placed in grade one, which was my placement prior to leaving North Carolina, I was placed back in kindergarten.

Paul was placed in the second grade rather than the third. That was not so much of a problem then, but it would become another thing for others to talk about once we returned to North Carolina approximately a year and a half later. I would be more than a year older than most of my peers throughout the remainder of my grade school years in North Carolina. Again, that should not have been such a major deal, yet it always seemed to be. No matter how clear the explanation for the age/grade discrepancy was, I was viewed with negative eyes by my peers. Such a perception by others would only serve to strengthen my already well-developed sense of being different and out of sorts.

In that kindergarten class in Camden, I remember our class visiting an apple orchard one day on a field trip. We were all lined up and given an apple at the end of the tour. While we were standing there in the orchard waiting to load up and return to school, I spotted a larger apple on the ground next to me. I dropped the one I had in my hand and picked up the more desirable one off the ground.

The boy behind peered around at me and said, "I'm gonna tell the teacher; you dropped that one and picked up another." I can see myself establishing firm eye contact with him and, without saying a word to him, making it clear to him that I really did not care. I was going to keep the second apple! I have often wondered why that incident with the student and the apple has remained so strongly with me.

Even though I was well indoctrinated into the abuse by then, there was still a part of me that was confident and secure within myself. Although I would lose the majority of that sense of self later, it's good to be able to look back and not see total darkness within and about me.

* * *

Meanwhile, back on the "Ponderosa," the landlord's big white house sat approximately 400 yards from where we stayed. He had a son named Johnny who treated us fairly nice – when it was just him. In fact, we often played together, primarily swinging Tarzan style on a rope attached to a big oak tree. Otherwise, Johnny would often hurl racial insults at us whenever his friends were around. I remember thinking that was an awfully strange and cruel way to treat people. I can recall Johnny and company chasing Paul and me through some woods one day. Somehow Paul and I became separated. Johnny and two of his friends caught up with me shortly after I made it back to the complex area. They showed me a knife with what appeared to be blood on it, and commented, "We've killed Paul." My heart sank and tears actually began to form as I stood staring at the knife.

Paul would round the corner about that time, though, sweating and breathing heavily from the chase. Johnny and his friends would roar with laughter as they turned and began making their way back toward the big white house.

Several years later, back in North Carolina, something similar would happen to me. This time six or seven of us had gone fishing several miles from our countryhood and had ended up getting lost because we chose not to backtrack when leaving. We caught very little, if anything, in the way of fish. We would end up walking seven or eight miles through a wooded area before finally coming onto the dirt road that was supposed to have been just a hop, skip, and a jump from the fishing location. But the two older guys, Donnie and Leroy immediately recognized where we were at that point and how far we had to travel to get home. While we made our way in the direction of the homestead, a black mustang would round the curve and pull up beside us. There were four white guys in the car. While hurling the standard racial slurs, nigger this and nigger that, one of them in the back seat flashed a small hand gun for us to see as anger flashed across our faces. We all froze when the gun appeared. No one said a word. We shot quick glances at one another. The pompous-ass grin on the white boy's face with the gun will probably be a permanent fixture with me.

Following the quick glances, we almost simultaneously bolted back into the woods. I could hear the white boys shut the engine off and get out of the car, they would begin to give chase, shouting at us at the same time. We quickly put distance between us and them. After having run approximately a mile or so, one of our guys, Willie P., nearly fell into a partially covered abandoned well, coming within inches of dropping down into the pit. Witnessing this near catastrophe, Donnie and Leroy stopped dead in their tracks and looked at each other. "Shi-i-t, the hell with this!" they would say nearly in chorus. Anger quickly replaced the fear. They each ripped separate limbs from a nearby tree and told the rest of us to "grab something." We would run no more!

The rest of us, including Willie P., armed ourselves with whatever piece of nature we could get our hands on. We then turned and headed back toward the road – and the white boys. Our nemeses spotted us from a distance approaching through the woods. Seeing that there was a new attitude about us, they would hurriedly scamper, gun and all, back to the black mustang. We would continue to carry our weapons for a few hundred yards after returning to the dirt road as we watched the black mustang disappear from view. When we were relatively sure that it would not return, we discarded the pieces of wood. Strangely enough, with assurance that we were safe, our old horse, Tom, long since deceased, popped into my mind. The flat bed wagon worked its way to memory consciousness as well. This was the same stretch of dirt road we had been on that Sunday afternoon with Tom.

***

While in New Jersey, the physical abuse at the hands of our father took the form of being beaten with belts, switches, lightweight apple limbs, etc., seemingly at the drop of a hat. Being whipped into that state of unconsciousness by him with that infamous 2 x 4 came about because I had made fun of the size of his penis. I had observed it while he slept one hot summer afternoon. The heat was smothering. The window was raised, the curtains drawn, and a gentle hot breeze filtered in and throughout the room. I don't remember why I even went into the room. I made the mistake of going over and mentioning how small it was to our duplex neighbor, who in turn went back to my father, laughing at him. I will never forget the question my father asked every time he struck my backside with the 2 x 4, as I was positioned on a bunk bed on my hands and knees: "How big is yours; how big is yours, boy?" his booming James Earl Jones,, Darth Vader baritone voice sounded out, over and over and over again. I would cry and scream for a while, but the board only seemed to contact my rear that much harder. After a while I just quit the vocalizations and took the pain. I would eventually pass out with him still swinging the 2 x 4. I do not remember waking up.

To my recollection, he never called me by name; it was always boy. "Boy, go get me a glass of water; boy, go bring that wood in: boy, sit you ass down over there and shut up". It is a good bet that this is partly the reason for the current fascination with my name: Curtis D. Wall. Our neighbors would make it a point after that not to tell my father anything that might bring his ire down upon either Paul or me. Even though they had probably seen my father lay hands on us before, the exhibition with the 2 x 4 stunned them also. As many times as I had been whipped, that time had been the worst. I never bothered asking if someone had encouraged him to stop, or if he had just worn himself out and then stopped.

I would steal a half dollar piece from that same duplex neighbor some time after that and return it to him when he confronted me about it. My father would step through the front door shortly after the incident and ask the question, "What's going on?" I would freeze immediately. My neighbor shot a quick glance my way, noticing the shear terror that had arisen within me. My neighbor would mention nothing about me having taken the coin, for he knew what was in store for me if he did. My father would commence small talk conversation with our neighbor after he responded with, "Nothing, he's (me) just hanging out here." I slowly turned my back to them and sat motionless until my father exited by the doorway. Even now, I continue to intermittently jump or flinch when unexpectedly touched in some way. As a side note, it is clear to me now that I was told "no" so often during those times that today I tend to preface any response during mostly informal conversations (unless I made a conscious effort not to do so), with "no."

There was another neighbor at that time who often interceded or tried to indirectly protect Paul and me from our father's wrath. We came to affectionately call him Uncle V. In addition to saving us from the whippings, he made the effort to teach us things he believed growing boys needed to know. We knew that he was very aware of our father falling short in that department. I admired the man and was grateful for him being in our world at that time. I owe him a great deal for taking time with us and for looking out for us. This would be the same gentleman that years later would introduce me to my first taste of alcohol (a Pabst Blue Ribbon beer, of which I could only drink a couple of swallows before becoming full and passing it back to Uncle V).

In between the episodes of abuse and the effort of trying to be a normal kid otherwise, I would be introduced, to some degree to my first sexual experience.

For the lower income, non-urban black community in those days, this was not that unusual an occurrence: the experimentation of sex based on what has been observed by the adults in our world; our 'child-interpretation' of normal, expected behavior. This particular experience is definitely more accurately assessed as 'pseudo sex' versus a true intercourse situation. Neither the girl, also around the age of seven, nor I knew what we were doing as we rolled around on top of one another in the '55 Studebaker one evening shortly after dusk. I don't remember who she was, the daughter of one of our neighbors perhaps? I simply don't remember. I do remember looking up from the young passionate session and thinking, "Why are the car windows so fogged up?" Of course, I have long since learned the answer to the question. I don't recall how or when the encounter ended; I don't recall ever seeing her again, though I am reasonably sure that I did.

The news of our being abused would again make it back to Grandma Wincy in North Carolina. But it would take more than a year of her threatening our father, I assumed with legal action, before he finally agreed to send us back to her. I suspect that my father grew tired of the responsibility of taking care of us.

I am sure that we cramped his lifestyle more than just a bit. Working with and for him in the fields gradually took a back seat. Also, back in North Carolina, my older brother and sister, Tom (actually James Thomas) and Emmie Lee, helped our cause by their persistent crying and pleading for Grandma to put pressure on our father to return us. Tom and Emmie Lee had a different father from Paul, Larry, Emmanuel, and me, but I remember that never making a difference to any of us. Though the words were never emotionally verbalized, we were brothers and sister.

In any event, major damage had already been forged upon our psyches. For Paul, the social part of life appeared on the surface, at least, to be easier. He tended to be more accepted by folks than I was when we returned to Morven, though his mental and emotional anguish would later destroy him. I would watch from a distance the obvious ease with which he seemed to become a part of those around him. I do not recall anyone ridiculing or making fun of him during those times. He did not stutter, nor did his physical appearance lend itself to being laughed at. He had a healthy set of teeth. I envied him.

The verbal abuse and occasional unprovoked physical attacks at the hands of peers and older guys became institutions throughout my (late) elementary and high school years. My head must have had a sign on it that said, " Smack me, please." It happened far too many times; there was seldom retaliation or defense on my part, especially after the age of 10. Between the pain and anger of what loomed large in my mind as being continually rejected by others, I would from time to time attempt to figure out why I was apparently so unlikable. Never was I able to come to any legitimate conclusion.

Michael E's comment my first day at school upon my return to Morven: "That boy sure has an ugly head," still lingers. Things and comments of that nature continued from that point on in terms of the schoolyard scene. For whatever reason, Michael E., backed off from the negative commentary about me shortly after that, and he and I eventually came to have mutual respect for one another throughout the remainder of our association.

I began to realize more and more a growing presence within me of feelings of fear and hatred for God, people and myself. I came to the point of resenting others I perceived as being more liked, more accepted and more appreciated than I was. Even now as an adult, this demon continues to rear its head from time to time, though in a much softer light. Almost always, this feeling comes during those times when I am depressed and doubting myself. I came to understand from others that I almost always had a mean, angry look on my face. I even got to the point where I would consciously make the effort to smile (without opening my mouth, of course) to not appear angry. Oftentimes, my perceived demeanor provided an avenue for others to expel their sickness. My Aunt Naomi would explain to a group of our relatives at a family function on one occasion that I was not angry, rather I was "just hurtin' inside." More accurate though, it was the hurt that had turned into anger. Aunt Naomi always seemed to have a special insight, a special awareness of what was happening with me emotionally and mentally. I grew to appreciate that ability about her more and more over the course of time.

* * *

My mind would eventually take on the traits of "The Secret Life of Walter Mitty" fantasies. I fantasized about being the knight in shining armor, about my being the ultimate defender of those done unjustly. I was their hero. How desperately I wanted someone, anyone, to be my hero, to be my protector. Those folks who saved me from probable abuse encounters with my father were seemingly not enough. My inner child was constantly afraid, insecure, and uncertain of what the world around him held. My fantasies about saving others were simply a subconscious reaction to my own developed feelings of being unloved, exposed and left out in the cold. Today, in my adult state, I will do unrelenting battle for those I feel have been unjustly wronged. I legitimately yearn to make such a difference. I truly have a difficult time sitting back idly watching another human being be abused and/or taken advantage of. Today, I have to reassure my inner child on a daily basis that I will be there for him. I may temporarily falter in my efforts to protect him, but I will never abandon him!

* * *

    Between the rages thrashing within me, there were some peaceful Moments and good times growing up. Those times usually came when I hung out with a small circle of folks, including my brother Larry, my cousin Tony, and friends of ours, Willie P., and Ray Charles. We would teach ourselves to swim in one of the local creeks minus any adult supervision, as well as hunt, catch, and eventually cook crawfish and bullfrogs. We'd batter and fry the legs. We'd search out and destroy (eat) wild berries such as blackberries, huckleberries, cherries, bullits (grapes), blueberries and raspberries. We'd pick wild plums and steal watermelons from distant neighbors; we enjoyed hanging out with one another.

    There would be times also when we stole bicycles from the local trading post, because our folks could not afford to buy them. We couldn't wait until March of every year when the weather turned warm, to discard our shoes and go barefoot through the Spring, Summer, and part of the Fall, when not in school or church. Play time also included our racing one another 40 to 50 yards on our hands and engaging in rousing games of full contact football – without pads.

    Good times for me, for there was rarely any of the regular abuse when I hung out with just that select group. I actually engaged in normal teasing and checking with those guys.

    We would just sit around and rap sometimes – about the future, about how things were one day going to be different for us. Such comments usually revolved around having the monies to do whatever we wanted to – one day. I fantasized out loud about the many wonderful things I was going to do; I would fantasize about this great and famous person I would at some point in my adult future be recognized as. The boys would glance at one another whenever my time came to share. One of them would invariably make the comment, "uh-oh, here goes Curtis off on this tangent, again." Tony would occasionally try to bring a little reality back to my visions. Sometimes even now I get confused about what is pure grandiosity versus what is me just having high expectations of myself. In any event, I am grateful for those times. Amidst the storms I was otherwise being confronted with, they were much needed distractions.

I would become acutely aware of the apparent ease with which Larry and Tony fit in socially with everyone. Much of my time around other people was spent with them in a variety of settings. Both commanded the respect of our peers and most of the older folds in our world at that time. I would stand back at times and watch their interaction with others and the way that they were accepted and be impressed and envious at the same time. What I didn't consciously acknowledge during those times was that Larry and Tony were relatively happy people and that is what they presented people with. They were real; they were genuine. I, on the other hand, was miserable through and through, and that is what I presented people with. It was obvious that I had no confidence in myself, and many folk chose to take advantage of that, perhaps to make themselves feel better about who they were.

I can feel good about the fact that rarely did I allow my feelings of jealousy for either Larry or Tony, to have me unfairly treat them or have me not go out of my way to help them obtain something they wanted that was within my limited power to assist them in achieving. I would even, at one point in high school, help Tony get together with a young lady who I was madly in love with myself. I wanted (BJ) badly, but it was evident that her thoughts of an intimate relationship were for Tony and not me. She was a cheerleader and one of the most popular folk in our senior class. BJ had an awesome spirit about her that was totally captivating. As painful as it was, I chose to accept the handwriting on the wall rather than to engage in useless attempts to secure BJ's affection for myself. I was proud of myself for being so reality-based. I did good.

    I am sure that if Tony had not been such a good person, my jealousy would have been more severe. He was and is a straight dude, treating other people squarely. My feelings toward him would have been more slanted simply since I often got tired of seeing him treated as the golden boy by the other fellows. He was the unofficial leader of the neighborhood clique and shined in just about every athletic sport he attempted. He also came from a home that had a mother and father. His family was not quite as bad as mine in terms of letting each other know they cared about one another. His family appeared to be more respected in the community. His last name was McRae; mine was Wall. There always seemed to be a majority who were less impressed with the latter. The view I had of myself did not help matters and was, perhaps the most critical agent in that equation.

2
Impacts

There are always people who are put into our lives to facilitate our survival. There are times when these significant others are obviously good and positive while they are working their magic on us. There are others who come across just the opposite at times. We allow them to create pain, to breed doubt in ourselves, to instill fear in us. If we are fortunate, a time will come when we mature to realize that those apparent negative forces were not real. They turn out to be very valuable learning opportunities for us.

There exists no such thing as a human being put on this planet for the sole purpose of experiencing and living in agony a lifetime (however that breaks down in individual chronological years), and then just rolling over and dying. There is a purpose for all the seeming madness. Our job is to hold on long enough, and allow those significant others to help us continue long enough to discover our true purpose. *In order to truly know the Light, one has to have experienced the Darkness.*

It is key to understand some of the terminology being used here. One in particular that deserves such focus is "allow". Severe and constant emotional pain may have us in a state of false denial on an everyday basis. No human being wants to hurt and suffer. Emotional and mental distress may have us telling ourselves that we don't care whether the agony is relieved or, in fact, whether we live or die.

The truth of the matter though, is that we do care! Below that initial surface of pain, we do care. No amount of delusionary thinking is going to change that. It is our responsibility, despite the level of pain, to allow others to fulfill part of their purpose for being on the planet – to help us know that there is hope for us.

We have the ability to manifest that control of our world, though at times this seems a great distance away.

No man is an island is certainly applicable to all of us. We certainly do not live in a vacuum. None of us, regardless of our degree of dysfunction or level of healthiness, can survive and reach a point of self-actualization without the assistance of other folks.

***

I can recall being hugged by only two people in my life up to the time that I reached 20 years of age. One of those people was Mrs. White, my first grade teacher. Mrs. White made it a point to give me and the other students a hug every morning as we entered her classroom. I treasure the image that I still carry in my head of Mrs. White wrapping her rather large arms around my small frame and pressing me against her well-endowed bosom, with a huge smile on her face. I remember her as being a heavy set, light-skinned woman with black hair streaked with gray. I felt loved; I felt protected – at those brief Moments. There would be no more hugs for me after leaving Mrs. White's class until years later.

Aunt Myrtle, whom I had not seen for a couple of months (because of my being away at college) walked up and hugged me one afternoon. She was that other individual. Aunt Myrtle had never hugged me before, yet she made it seem natural. That same warm and protected feeling returned. Oftentimes when I reflect upon those two interludes in my life, there is a mixture of both happiness and sadness. I feel fortunate to have received even that much physical affection, yet I am also saddened by the lack of such attention not coming from others, principally my own family.

Today, I maintain a serious passion for the hug, even though my still sometimes cool demeanor would deny that. Stored away in the back of my mind is the notion that needing physical and, especially, emotional fulfillment in the form of a hug is unmanly. In reality, the opposite is true. A real man does not ignore or choose to forego his genuine emotional state because of a faulty societal creed. I get angry with myself sometimes because I feel I need that brand of emotional security too much. I occasionally forget that the path of emotional growth and healing is a continuous work in progress.

* * *

The stuttering problem would set upon me when I entered the fourth grade. It had not been evident before. To this day, the primary explanation I have been able to formulate in my mind as to why the condition hit me then is that things of a socially prevalent nature (girls, peer pressure, increased expectations, etc.) arrived at that time. I am also aware that severe emotional and/or physical abuse oftentimes plays a significant role in the development of speech difficulty. Nearly every time I had to read or speak in class I would stutter. Most of my classmates would laugh and usually I would cry. Even in Sunday School, there was no escape from the snickers when it came my time to read. I remember thinking, surely I must be a bad lot if folks laughed at me in church, God's House. There could be no relief anywhere then.

The teasing came about the shape of my head ("egghead") and the deformity of my two front teeth, which were bucked, cavity-ridden and gapped from earlier years of sucking my thumb and not brushing them on a regular basis. As far as the shape of my head was concerned, it simply was not cool back during those times with the childish mentality that ruled our world, to have an elongated head. There were occasions when I sought to show an air of self-acceptance about my head. I would go to the board during one of those classroom down-periods, draw a football-shaped head and highlight that critical "point" with the word brain. I was indicating to my peers the reason for my acknowledged intelligence was because of the extra head mileage, specifically that "point". Of course, the teacher would be out of the class during those times. In fact, I dreaded those times when the teacher left us alone for any extended period of time. I knew that it would be just a matter of time before someone focused their attention on me in a negative way. Such Moments rarely failed to materialize.

After crying on many of those occasions, I would turn to fighting anyone and everyone who made fun of me. To this day, blindsided spontaneous laughter creates Momentary havoc within me. Almost always though, I would be the one scolded by the teacher or sent to the principal's office, enhancing even more that sense of injustice that was already in me. Eventually, I would stop the fighting and retaliations, and just take it. I had now consciously begun to shut myself off from everyone and everything – when it was not necessary for me to be actively involved. I am sure that I could have handled any regular negative happenstances.

However, the combination of all of these unpleasant circumstances, coupled with the abuse suffered earlier at the hands of my father, and Mom dying and leaving me, made things nearly unbearable for me then – and for years to come.

I began to daydream more and more, thinking about how things might one day be different for me, being happy and at peace with myself. In the meantime, pain, anger, fear and self-pity reigned supreme in my world. I would eventually come to believe that I had been born into this world as someone to be abused to make others feel better about themselves. By the time I had entered the fifth grade, in spite of the ongoing teasing, I was falling in love with the young ladies…and being rejected by them just as quickly. Tears from what seemed to be constant dismissal by my female peers would come on occasions. Nobody loves me would become more ingrained in me with each perceived rejection.

Drawing and sketching had become a passion for me by the time I entered the fourth grade. By all accounts, I was very good at it. I would draw, mostly pictures of people nearly ever chance I got, in and out of school. I knew even then that the drawing provided a time of solace for me. When I sketched, I became lost in the challenge of bringing something or someone to life on paper. I used to keep a notebook binder that included my better efforts and special efforts. No one laughed at me when my art ability came up. Toward the end of my fifth grade year, I would grow disillusioned even with my drawing. I would end up giving my notebook of drawings to one of my classmates who jumped at the opportunity to acquire them. I remember the stunned look on Willie James Perkins' face when I actually placed the binder in his hands. I never drew for pleasure again after that day. Periodically, through the years, I would only sketch when it would be a necessary part of some overall project I was working on.

During my middle school years I had a serious passion for one young lady in particular. For the most part, she tolerated my subtle and ineffective overtures of affection. Usually when it was just the two of us in one of those rare isolated Moments, she tended to treat me nice. I now can see she actually liked me but could not allow herself to commit to being my girlfriend. Surely she would have suffered teasing and probable rejection from her female friends. This young lady when in the presence of those girlfriends, could be just as cruel as the rest of them. On one occasion, over a three to four day period she led me to believe that she was seriously considering a relationship with me, but one of her friends laughingly told me the object of my affection had played me like a fine-tuned instrument and that I had fallen for it hook, line and sinker. "Egg thinks I like him," was supposedly the comment she had made to the girls after a time of humoring me. With that revelation my heart sank to a new low.

At home I was becoming angry and resentful at being asked, told and/or made to do things, primarily routine chores. Some of my family members would also occasionally make fun of my stuttering and physical appearance. Things became so out of sorts for me that I attempted to run away from home. I only made it about a mile from the house before I decided to take refuge in a field. My Aunt Marie and younger brother, Larry, came looking for me where I was hiding. Aunt Marie then proceeded to drag me back home with one arm while whipping me with the other. Of course, the next day at school, Larry made sure that everybody knew about my "running-away escapade" the night before. At least that gave me a break from the "usual" things I was normally chided about ... for a day anyway.

One day at school I was visited by a speech therapist, who was to assess and (hopefully) provide some measure of treatment for my stuttering condition. The white lady, along with my fifth grade teacher, Mrs. Johnson, took me to an empty classroom. She requested and listened to me read a sentence, and then uttered to Mrs. Johnson, "He sure does have a bad problem." The therapist then took me back to my regular classroom, said good-bye, and I would never hear from her again. I guess she didn't think much of me either. But amidst the "rejection" from that particular incident, something in me rose up and I promised myself then that one day I would again speak without stuttering … and I would do an exceptional job at it. During that disappointing Moment, I remembered that I had not always been that way. The third grade Christmas Program flashed through my mind, where I was standing on the stage in the school auditorium before the entire elementary student body delivering a memorized holiday message with poise, confidence, and realness. There was little fear or nervousness; there was no stuttering.

I must give praise and thanks to God for sending Mrs. Johnson into my world at that time. In addition to her concern about my stuttering, she exuded a quiet and genuine compassion for me as a person. The biggest gift I remember her bestowing upon me during that year that I spent with her was simply treating me just like she did everybody else. She made no distinction between me and my classmates, in spite of my perceived shortcomings when I compared myself to the other students.

Mrs. Johnson was firm and had high expectations of all of us. She would very seldom yell, but everyone knew that several licks from a car fan belt in the palm of our hand was coming if we had blatantly dissed her or intentionally not followed through on those more than routine homework assignments. But throughout the firmness and the occasional corporal punishment, most of us knew that she truly cared. Mrs. Johnson also had two gorgeous daughters in their late teens or early twenties, who would periodically stop by during the course of the school year and visit their mother and hang out with us for a couple of hours at a time. The young ladies often danced with us, showing us the latest hip-hop dance steps, as well as teaching us to waltz and two-step. I envied the loving relationship they obviously had with their Mom. Though nearly always emotionally cool, Mrs. Johnson was still noticeably very proud of them. The confidence and social ease were never there for me to fully engage in the dance movements the young ladies practiced with us. I was too caught up into being stared at and laughed at. My self-consciousness ruled the house.

I felt pressured to attend the occasional school dances. I would never get to go with the person I wanted to, often allowing myself to be pressured into taking someone else. I played the wall flower role to the max. At no time did I ever hit the dance floor, even with the girl that I had taken! Of course, that would create more for the other kids to harp on at me about. Oh, how I really wanted to be out there on the dance floor. I remember the music sounding good and most folks having fun. I was scared to death. I am sure that it showed throughout every ounce of my being. My date would become angry and seek refuge and active participation with someone else. The staring and the talk about me generally took on a much harsher tone at that point. I would be embarrassed and help them beat myself up even more.

Three other teachers would play significant roles in my world later as well.

The first was Mr. Hunter, who taught me 9th grade Science. Mr. Hunter generally said very little to me on an individual basis. He would usually direct his opinions to the whole class when returning test papers. He let it be known that he thought I was intelligent and a good student. Mr. Hunter communicated this on more than one occasion without ever calling my name directly, but everyone in the class knew he was alluding to me. I generally made the highest grades on tests and quizzes. Mr. Hunter's comments made me feel good about myself – for that Moment, though I resisted feeling good about myself for too long. I knew it wouldn't last anyway.

Ms. Lewis, who taught me English and Journalism, refused to let me hide in the shadows. She would intentionally assign projects to me that would put me in front of the class. Ms. Lewis knew how much I dreaded such tasks, and I'm pretty sure she knew why I dreaded such attention. Ms. Lewis never questioned me about what I was going through or what I may have been through. She would let me know indirectly on more than one occasion that the past did not matter and that I had to somehow believe in myself in the Moment. Ms. Lewis' compassion and belief in me shone ever so brightly. The other students were aware of the special effort she put forth with me. Several of them made attempts to follow suit as well. But, as was my well developed state of being by then, I would only allow any of them to lift me up but on a limited basis. There were several times when I saw the disappointment in this lady when I would "passively-aggressively" refuse her attempts to help me.

Mrs. Randle taught me Algebra. As with Mr. Hunter, she had very little to say to me on a personal level. I remember her looking at me at various times with expressions of support, understanding, and at times admiration. She had a smile about her that dictated to me that everything was going to be okay. I knew she felt my pain; I knew she cared. At no time would she allow us students to check or put one another down. I remember her having very few disciplinary problems in her classroom. She was not loud or threatening; in fact, she very seldom raised her voice above a normal conversational tone. The respect was such for her because she exuded belief in all of us. We knew that teaching was more than just a job to her. I thank her for the non-verbal warmth she showed me on an almost daily basis. I believe (now) in my heart that Mrs. Randle genuinely liked me, above and beyond feeling sorry for me.

* * *

1966 brought with it the "Afro" craze, coming home to roost in my neighborhood. It would turn out to be a very unpleasant part of my sixth grade experience – and beyond. Everybody grew an Afro and wore it with immense pride. I attempted to grow one also, wanting to be like everyone else. But no matter how hard I tried to grow that Afro, it would not come. Part of the problem appeared to be related to a ringworm condition on the back left side of my head – that was healed by grade six, but hair would grow at a much slower rate there than the rest of my head. It also became clear to me during my first year in college that a constant state of anxiety had contributed greatly to my hair not growing normally. I was not strong enough at times to weather the nearly constant humiliation heaped upon me because of the "no fro". I would grow more and more closed within.

I would beg out of the valedictorian address at my eighth grade graduation because of a growing fear of people and that infamous stuttering condition. A fellow classmate, Marion K., would do the honors. I convinced myself to be content with the knowledge that the teachers and my peers knew that I had achieved that academic status. And that even though I could not find the courage to deliver the address, it was okay. I liked being viewed as smart and intelligent then, even though to this day I still have difficulty accepting that fact. The intermittent praise from teachers and peers allowed me to see some measure of light within myself. I would actively seek to do well in my schoolwork in order to receive that positive attention. That, plus the accolades I received for being a pretty good athlete back then as well as during high school and college years, were definitely soul boosters for me.

I became even more aware during that time also about the difference in terms of my motivation to do/accomplish tasks at home versus at school. As noted earlier, I resented having to do work at home. I know that part of the resistance to chores at home is typical of children and adolescents, but I firmly believe also that my resentments at home were more than the norm. Having had hard labor forced upon me by my father was one of two things that contributed greatly to my negative view of work at home. The other thing was the different levels of motivation. I received no praise at home for anything I did, whether it was beyond the call of duty or not. It was just the opposite from my teachers. With every ounce of praise I received, I wanted just that much more of it. Most of all though, I just wanted to feel loved and appreciated.

While one part of me was mired in resistance to authority, the other part of me was engulfed in not wanting to make anyone angry. The truth of the matter was, even though I was being eaten up with hurt and anger, I would go to great lengths to avoid conflicts – when not at home. Much of this went back to my own abuse and to my being in the presence of my father's abusive behavior toward my Mom and brother. While into people-pleasing I was, but at the same time I was having difficulty conforming to and being like everybody else. I would go out of my way to be different, but also strongly sought acceptance from others.

I am now aware of the fact that me never coming to know me, never coming to accept me, never coming to love me made it impossible at that time to consistently risk being who I was – out of a fear of being rejected by others. As time continued, I grew more angry with myself and less angry with people, because I had allowed myself to be abused; I should have been able to stop it; I should have been able to handle it better. Of course, during the earlier stages of my life, that was not reality at all.

* * *

Prior to my entering high school, I worked a summer job picking peaches.

As had been the pattern of my life up to that point, the negative experiences with that particular venture far outweighed the positive. We would be packed in a camper-covered pick-up truck around 6:00 a.m. on weekdays and occasionally on Saturdays when the peach crop was on overload and had to be picked. Just riding to and from the worksite was a harrowing daily experience for me. "That boy looks like a scared rabbit," a light-skinned girl about my age said one afternoon on the ride home. I recall throwing a quick glance in her direction, making Momentary eye contact. It almost appeared to me as if she were angry with me for being so self-deprecating and so unsure of myself. When her words registered with me, there was no denying that her perception of me was accurate. I hated the fact that she was right. That particular evening was one of the longest rides home of that summer.

Impacts

The grown-ups with whom I worked during that summer were impressed with my work ethic. While I was able to be appreciative somewhat of the adults' favorable view of me, I really wanted the approval and acceptance of my peers. I watched how several of the guys worked their magic in getting along with folks, particularly with the young ladies. Oh, how I envied them, wanting to be that self-confident, wanting to be that well-liked and accepted by the masses. I would dread lunch hour each day, for it was time I did not have work as an excuse not to interact with others. Lunchtime was also the time when the perceived great disparity between my social skills and the more popular guys became blatantly obvious. More often than not I found a corner, ate my sandwich or bag of chips with measured anxiety and my back to as many folk as possible. Then I usually just stood and watched the others expressing themselves with little noticeable difficulty, dancing and high-fiving. If I had not been in need of the money and if all the other boys were not working the peach orchards that summer, I would have opted not to put myself through that. To say I was glad when that particular summer stretch ended would be an understatement!

I thank God for instilling in me, in spite of the abuse and development of negative self-image, a strong desire to achieve and somehow be more than just among the status quo. As noted earlier I did well academically, to include Science and English awards and membership in the Honor Society in high school. During my high school career I would letter in football, track and cross-country as well. It was the general consensus among many that I was a pretty good athlete, in spite of myself. I knew I had more ability; I knew I was more capable – but nowhere in my heart and soul did I believe it. I was just mentally and emotionally screwed-up to perform well consistently. Even though the need to do something to get positive feedback from others was a part of it, there was more to it. I think back sometimes about how many afternoons I would have to hitchhike from school after a practice, and the several times I even walked the 13 mile distance after becoming tired of waiting for someone to pick me up. My family did not own a car during those times, so I did what I had to do.

I played organized football for the first time as a sophomore in high school.

I remember being put down at home a few times, occasionally sarcastically being called the big man because I was adamant about playing football, something no one else in the family had done before. The majority of the guys on that year's team had been playing since grade school. I was intimidated even more because of that. The only experience I brought to the table was having played sandlot tackle football, without the benefit of pads of course, with the fellows on numerous occasions. I would hold my own for the most part on the high school squad. I would break my collar bone one afternoon making a tackle in practice. Head Coach H., who was black, would show some initial concern for the injury, instructing me to go to the locker room to get dressed – for the trip to the emergency room.

I would emerge from the locker room, after struggling to shower and dress, with my shirt simply draped over my shoulders. My clavicle or collarbone would be swollen by this time. I was informed by one of the assistant coaches that Coach H., had left. As I stand there stunned and feeling worthless, the assistant Coach turns and walks away as well. Moments after stirring myself around, I would head for the hospital on my own – walking. Mack H., a teammate, and his parents who actually lived in the opposite direction of the hospital would pick me up from the highway and transport me to the emergency room. They would hang around while the hospital staff did what they had to do, and take me to my home, still 10 – 11 miles away. My eternal gratitude to Mack and his folks, who were white, for going out of their way to help me that day.

I would remain at home for a couple of days and a weekend before returning to school. Coach H., never offered any explanation for having left me at school that afternoon. He barely established eye contact with me when he spoke to me after that. I remember the feelings of unworthiness, unlovableness that intensified in me. I believed at the time that if I had been one of the coach's star players, he would have personally made the effort to make sure my injury was medically addressed. But I was not one of his star players. What he and his coaching staff did was unthinkable for any responsible adults to do. I would return to the team in time to participate in the final game of the season. The majority of the guys were accepting of me, but I never felt a part of the team. I knew that was more my fault than theirs. Coach H., would end up moving to Ohio before the school year ended. I knew from others talking that he had some things going on in his personal life that were heavy. I knew that I should not have taken his treatment of me personally, but I did.

Also, as a part of the Coach H., era I had been given an opportunity to possibly run the ball some, but my non-performance in practice one day nixed that idea in a hurry. Being aware that I had better than average speed, the coaches had asked me to go back and field a few kick-offs. Out of a sense of fear and a lack of confidence, I intentionally overshot or undershot each ball that came to me. After about the fourth time of not catching the ball, the coaches shook their heads and asked me to move down to the other end of the field – with the lineman; I weighed 117 pounds at the time. I had blown my chance at perhaps garnering a more appropriate position for me since I had the necessary speed and quickness to more than get the job done. I hated me for it. Whether it was football, track and field, or later in cross country and wrestling, a great deal of natural athletic talent was squandered and never brought to the show.

During the summer of 1973, I began to lose my teeth with increasing rapidity due to a well-developed state of pyorrhoea. I would accidentally break my upper partial plate during wrestling practice one afternoon. Because of the immediate lack of money and transportation, I super glued the broken tooth back onto the partial plate frame. I would wrestle no more; my coach at that time would look at me with a combination of pity and disgust when I told him about my decision to quit the team and why I was quitting. I would walk around with the partial in that condition for approximately a year before eventually having the plate replaced.

That experience, combined with the stuttering condition, only served to further strengthen my phobia about not eating or talking in public unless absolutely necessary. Several other dental plates were to follow over the course of years, finally having my last nine permanent teeth removed at the age of 38 and replaced with a full set of dentures.

* * *

It was also during that junior year that I became obsessed with consistently wearing some sort of head gear, to hide my head and hair, or lack of hair - head gear was not allowed at school. Nor would I wear a hat to church, but almost at no other times was I caught without something on my head. My picture as a part of my high school cross country team would fail to appear in the yearbook for my senior year because I refused to be photographed without my standard toboggan. The photographer, as well as members of the cross country team, found a great deal of humor in my resistance that day. I found no humor in the situation, only more embarrassment, more humiliation.

I entered college later wearing a modified, homemade sweat band daily during the initial two months of the first semester. I had gone to that, following my stint with the toboggan, and a red and white railroad cap with the top cut out and the edge re-hemmed. During the Fall, my track coach would ask me in an exasperated tone, after not having seen me without the headband on since my arrival on campus, "Do you always wear that thing on your head?" I do not remember what my verbal response was, but I do recall feeling embarrassed by the question, particularly since there were other student athletes present. It would be shortly after that encounter that I would abandon the headband. Because of the broadness of the campus and my knowing few folk there, and few folk knowing me at that time, some of the anxiety within me would subside and my hair would begin to grow. I actually grew an Afro!

Besides positive stroking from select individuals, I would categorize grades 4 – 12 as basically miserable times for me. I quickly grew to the point of loathing going to school, because I knew the barrage of put-downs that awaited me. I would count down the days to Friday when I would receive a break from that particular environment. At school, the jokes and the ridicule seemed larger than life, mostly due to the fact that I was in a confined environment and could not leave, at least I chose not to leave. I regret not having fostered some relationships that could have been very positive since I had failed at my attempts with others. I regret not having attended my high school prom, supposedly one of the more memorable events in one's high school experience.

At one point, I developed and harbored much disdain for my black race as a whole. Please do not misunderstand me, I am very proud of my heritage; I would not trade my heritage for any other if given the opportunity. But it was from my own people that I was presented with the more gut wrenching experiences with pain and rejection. I understand very well that much of that is true because I hung around mainly black folk. The white folk generally did not bother me, more than likely due to general discomfort created by the color difference. I didn't realize it at the time, but there were several peers, black and white that actually thought a lot of me. I will always remember the last day of school during my 12th grade year when a couple of those peers made it a point to tell me how much they respected me. In my heart, I truly did not believe that they were sincere, but I appreciated the sentiments. I have come to grips with the my-people issue, realizing that those negative things heaped upon me were merely situations in time, a part of my evolutionary training. The perceived cruelty extended by my peers and by those gravely immature adults was normal, given the unnatural nature of the human being.

3
(No) Sex, Drugs and the Blues

Because I lacked self-love and self esteem, and because I wanted to avoid as much ridicule and criticism as possible or get hurt emotionally, I allowed no one to get really close to me. A part of me though hungered for the small group intimacy of a close circle of friends. I was nearly ravenous, on the other hand, for that interpersonal relationship as well. Again, the ladies who came to be the objects of my passion and desire would continuously make it clear to me that they only wanted to be friends. Of course, I blamed their rejection of me on my physical appearance and the stuttering condition. This became standard with me: "If I couldn't have who I wanted then I did not want anyone else." My inability to give up that ideal has oftentimes dumbfounded me, for surely I should have perhaps been willing to accept whatever positive and intimate attention anyone was willing to bestow upon me. There were times out of desperation and need of emotional and physical fulfillment that I settled for other than what I really wanted, but those associations would turn out to be short-term and, in the long run, not nearly satisfying enough.

In addition to carrying crushes (back and forth) for a couple of young ladies from elementary school days and BJ, a beautiful creature named SL captivated my attention during my senior year in high school. She had one of those "medium-sized" afros that seemed to be perfectly teased every day. The mini-skirts she wore frequently revealing the most perfect pair of legs I had ever encountered did nothing to deter my thoughts and desires at all. She was brown-skinned, with a dazzling smile, and had a good and kind heart to boot ... and I was in love – again. She would tell me in a letter once that while she was no longer fond of the guy that she had recently been dating, she did not want me – in that way. She liked me and had no problem being my friend; but that was it. I was crushed as I read the words. They would penetrate me like tiny daggers, in continuous succession until I finished the letter; and afterwards. I remember being somewhat surprised that the rejection bothered me so much. It had happened so many times in the past I thought I should be accustomed to it by then, thus, less affected. That was not the case. It never would be the case.

I officially remained a virgin until the age of 21, my junior year in college. If I could have had sex prior to that with whom I wanted to, I am relatively sure I would have. It was not out of a sense of virtue that I did not. I had little self-confidence to even set the stage for a sexual encounter of my choosing. My lack of sexual experience and very few real opportunities proved to be another avenue of ridicule for the boys to seize upon. In our world back then, our manhood was measured primarily by two things: 1) the ability to get a girl, to include having sex with her; and 2) the ability to consume and handle alcohol. I would fail miserably on both counts.

Drinking was a way of life in my community. If you were a man, you were expected to drink. Paul had long since fed into that system of thinking and started to pay the price early in his drinking career. He quickly developed the label of alcoholic in the neighborhood. He had also become known for having emotional fits when drunk. I got to witness one such episode. Paul, in a drunken stupor, was crying uncontrollably. Some guy had a shotgun pointed at him. Paul would keep saying over and over – between the tears, "Shoot me! Shoot me! I don't care; Shoot me!" The man, mumbling expletives to himself, would lower the gun and walk away. My mind would flash back to New Jersey and him sitting on that woodpile. My heart ached for him. But his time to die was to come later. Eerily that evening I saw me in him, as I had seen me in him many times before, especially during our last stay in New Jersey Paul and that evening was in actuality a vivid forecast of what lay ahead of me.

***

The first time I got drunk occurred during the summer of 1974, the year I graduated from high school. The boys had broken into a little country store and stolen crackers, candies, and Schlitz Malt Liquor Bull. I had received many invitations before to participate, but had always declined. I accepted this invitation. I was an avid participant in the festivities. I drank and ate and drank some more.

I experienced marijuana for the first time, vomited, went into a blackout and challenged a couple of boys to a fight – regarding comments they had made about me days earlier (told to me later, as I had no recollection of the incidents). The challenging of the guys was significant because – up until that Moment, I had not fought back or tried to defend myself against anybody for any of the ridicule and verbal abuse heaped upon me since the fourth grade.

I remember clearly how I felt having that second can of Schlitz Malt Liquor go down. Not so much the warm feeling in my chest as it was the intense and sudden confidence I felt. It was the first time in my life I had consciously recognized any within, false though it was. I felt like a junior god; I knew everything about everything. I was the life of the party, and I did not stutter a single time after having caught that initial buzz. During the recuperating period afterwards, a little voice inside whispered that I was bound for the world of alcoholism; I shut it down quickly. It would be years later though before I would mentally and verbally acknowledge such a state of being.

The most important thing for me then was that I had found something to take away the pain – if only for a little while. Over the course of the next ten years, alcohol and other drugs would provide that temporary relief for me. It would also push me to the brink of insanity. I remember during the party's aftermath that summer afternoon in 1974, after coming back to myself, one of the boys commented to another: "Did y'all see Curtis? Man, he was tore-up;

he was cool." For that brief Moment, I was finally one of the boys! I had made it! I was accepted!

I would spend what seemed like a lifetime after that trying to maintain that acceptance.

I do not remember drinking regularly the remainder of that summer, primarily because I was running and training almost daily, preparing for the upcoming cross country season at Wingate College where I had been accepted. Those occasional times I did drink with the boys, almost always the situations would develop into scenes where I was fighting or expressing a desire to fight someone. The built-up anger over the years would spill out, with me usually being in a blackout. Of course, I would have to suffer the ridicule and other accompanying consequences of those actions. Much of it was hard to live down. Some of it I have never been able to live down. Even after years I still maintain somewhat legendary status back in my hometown.

***

I met a young lady who was charged with keeping the local junior high gym open during that summer to provide a place of recreation for the young people. She had just completed her freshman year at Pembroke University. She was white and her family was well known and respected in the Morven community. Her name was Inez. We had the same last name – Wall; and there was an immediate attraction, a heart to heart attraction. We were truly linked souls and both of us knew that we were. I am convinced today that linked souls intuitively recognize one another, whether that association is brief and seasonal or otherwise, we know! Our friendship was real; the friendship was genuine. I believe to this day that my meeting her was divine intervention. Nothing sexual would ever come up throughout the course of our relationship. She was struggling with the ups and downs of her boyfriend at the time. A boyfriend, by the way, that she would eventually marry. I would listen when she needed to talk; she would listen when I needed to talk. There were much deeper issues of self and identity that we shared as well. We proved to be a comforting source for one another (she probably more so to me). Though we have talked and visited with each other minimally since 1979, that special bond still exists between us. Even now, we continue to refer to each other as "brother" and "sis. "Looking back with a clearer view of things, I can see that a cousin of mine cared a great deal about me also. Constance and I had always seemed to share a special closeness. The like-souls tenet is certainly applicable again. I felt and knew that she was going through some continuing emotional struggles with her own immediate family. I knew that she was also struggling with self, purpose, and identity. For the most part, she did exceptionally well at not revealing her true level of emotional pain. We would both be adults before Constance would share with me the magnitude of those struggles. Though I could not recognize it then, Constance had always tended to accept me – just as I was. I can remember feeling more comfortable around her than I was with other people. She would say later that she had a tremendous amount of respect and admiration for me. I was her role model! Can you imagine that? I certainly could not, until more recent times. I realize even more now that she was another one of those very special people God placed in my world to ensure, in spite of the darkness, my survival.

***

My two years at Wingate College proved to be a mixture of both positive and negative experiences for me. On the plus side, I received numerous accolades for my academic/literary skill ("Outstanding Black Student Graduate" Award; Phi Theta Kappa (honorary academic society) membership; Graduation Marshall; "Who's Who Among American Junior Colleges," President of the Black Student Organization; Sigma Alpha Omega (honorary math society) membership; "Outstanding Minority Talent Roster Listee of 1976"; Journalism Award – Sports Writing, to name a few). I was well thought of by most of my professors and the college administrators. I would make a 4.0 GPA during my first semester there. That seemed to impress students and administrators alike. I did not view it as a big deal then, but I inwardly enjoyed the positive attention that came along with such a feat. I remember it being more of a big deal to others because I was Black. That part of the experience angered me a great deal. Though I would flounder emotionally back and forth a part of me decided after that reaction the first semester, I would prove to the white folks that my demonstrated academic prowess was no fluke. I was an intelligent human being, regardless of the color of my skin.

Having taught myself to shoot billiards the hard way (playing for money from the outset) years earlier back in Morven, I enjoyed the reputation on campus as being a better than average pool player. There would occasionally be crowds in the rec room in the evenings to watch me play. And yes, I enjoyed the positive attention. I became known as deadly on the foosball table. I would do well in the campus tournaments in both recreational events up until the semi-finals, where the caliber of competition stiffened – and more eyes were upon me. I would spend more time worrying about what the spectators were thinking about and my appearance than I did focusing on the matches themselves. My self-consciousness was again defining who I was not.

I had some folks convinced that I knew karate. After months of tolerating a fellow student's obnoxious behavior (primarily toward others) because of his TaeKwonDo Brown Belt status, I challenged him to a sparring match. This guy would routinely threaten other students, those he perceived as being weaker. I had simply got fed up with the bullshit he dispensed onto others. (Look out! Here comes Mr. Walter Mitty to the rescue!) I made my way to one of the designated dorm rooms following track practice on the selected day. Word had got around campus about the challenge match; the hallway was lined wall to wall with people when I entered. Recalling my knowledge from a book that I had read on karate techniques, I thoroughly embarrassed the young man! Though he would return home to Winston Salem that weekend for update lessons from an older brother, to my knowledge, no one on campus ever had another problem with him! Because of such a negative past, I had little trouble handling the affirmative strokings. Though I played it cool, I wanted them; in fact, I needed the affirmations about self.

    The noted actor, Vincent Price, upon a visit to the college, would approach me during a reception at the Wingate College President's house following a general address in the campus auditorium. Everyone else had crowded around him while I stood back observing the scene. Mr. Price would glance over in my direction and after a few minutes, excused himself from the crowd (mostly student presidents of clubs/organizations on campus and faculty members), walked over, shook my hand, and introduced himself to me, as if I didn't know who he was. He smiled and chatted with me for a few minutes about my life and times at Wingate College before turning his attention to the school's President. The other guests would observe Mr. Price's undivided attention to me with wonderment. I knew in my heart that Mr. Price had only made such an effort because he had noticed my being the only minority student there and showing my discomfort with the situation in the process. I was grateful for such an effort on his part. If he had not already been one of my favorite actors at that time, he would have become one! I was impressed with his humanity, kindness, insight and observation. I never forgot that Moment. Not so much because of his legendary status as an actor, for I am truly not easily impressed because of a human being's elevated position in life, but because of him not having allowed his ego to forget the needs of others less elevated.

    My people pleasing mode was definitely in effect, and I was careful to present the model student demeanor during daylight hours. It's not that I faked being a good student, but rather I would not allow myself to be honest about my thoughts and feelings when I felt those significant others might take offence to them. I would even force myself to attend church on campus nearly every Sunday, simply because I knew many of my professors would be there and that they would look favorably on my being there. I would feel guilty for going to God's House not for the primary purpose of being spiritually fed and paying homage to the Supreme Creator.

Nevertheless, I would play the role during my stay at Wingate. It was a role that I took no pride in.

I genuinely liked most of my professors at Wingate – not just because they communicated the same to me. There were two who took the time to get to know me. I knew that they were pulling for me – to survive. In addition to fair treatment in the classroom, they also exhibited compassion beyond requirement. Much Love, Much Respect.

The folks that I hung out with after dark came to know another side of me. It was the side of me that drank excessively and smoked dope whenever I had the opportunity. They also became aware of my fragile emotional condition that would almost always show up in grand style whenever I reached a certain stage in my consumption of alcohol. The uncontrollable tears would inevitably come, along with an occasional threat of suicide.

The guys would look at me with pity, amazement and occasional disgust.

To my knowledge, they never spread the news of those far too frequent outbursts around campus. For that I was grateful. I believe that those guys, the Raeford (N.C.) gang – Al, Tyrone, Blue, Buie – looking at me carry on so, made them take a hard look at themselves "Curtis is a crazy, intelligent guy," is how my second-year roommate, Rickey L., described me during a newspaper interview. I knew exactly what he meant by the words. While there was little doubt that I was gifted intellectually, Rickey had seen a dark side of me time and time again, particularly during my sophomore year when we actually shared living quarters. He had witnessed the drunken stupors, the blackouts, and heard the ramblings of threats to end my life, in addition to the other outbursts that illuminated my very shaky emotional state.

He genuinely liked me in spite of my extreme moods and erratic behavior. I could tell he felt pity for me at times; I could tell also that he felt powerless to do anything to help me. Rickey and I both ran on Wingate's cross country and track teams, so he got to know me pretty well. He was willing to accept me as I was.

As things would turn out, Rickey and I have remained in contact throughout the years since Wingate. He is a true friend.

In those big track and cross country meets, I would set myself up for failure by intentionally partying heavily and getting only a couple of hours of sleep the night before. I would have an excuse if I lost. Someone once said, "Every ego has its favorite tool of sabotage, a particular ploy it uses to cloud the approach to light." The confidence and the deserving to win attitude simply were not there. Not enough had changed since my high school athletic days. I would know exactly what I was doing and why I was doing it, but could not or did not choose to use the capacity to do anything differently. I wanted to win, to do well, but the fear of failure and no belief in self stifled any consistent demonstration of that athletic ability.

I did have a girlfriend, LB, for part of that second year there. We never engaged in sexual intercourse, just heavy petting – as my mind was often filled with confusion and there was a serious unwillingness to trust my basic instincts. There was also a perceived lack of place and appropriate opportunity, but perhaps the most telling thing about the no sex item is that I was truly caught up in my having the opportunity to mentally and emotionally wrap myself around someone of my choosing, and having that person, LB, reciprocate those thoughts and feelings.

To me LB was a beautiful young lady, though her eyes were oftentimes contrastingly sad when she flashed that gorgeous smile of hers. The relationship would end after a couple of months as quickly as it had begun. I knew in my heart that she had also wanted to make love but had never broached the issue.

We had, however, temporarily filled an emotional void in each of us. Perhaps that was all there was supposed to have been to it. From my human, analytical eye, in looking back, I think that she grew tired of playing the good girl role, for she was truly not convinced she was good.

My Wingate memoirs also include SW, a white student I met during my second year there. SW and I would get drunk at least a couple of times a week, depending on what we both had going on after hours. I still occasionally hung out with the Raeford gang, but not as often as I had during freshman year. Anyway, I would ride with SW up to a local ABC store about a half-mile from campus.

We would drink mostly wine. SW was small in physical stature, wore glasses and appeared not to have many acquaintances. One night we would get stopped by one of Wingate's finest because SW had been weaving across the road. My heart nearly jumped from my chest when I realized we were going to be stopped, with nearly a half gallon of wine still left – and no way to get rid of it, since the officer was directly behind us by the time we saw him.

The officer would give me an option of going down town with him and SW or going on about my business, since I was not driving the car. My lofty status and reputation as a Wingate elite dominated my thinking. I would step from the car without mumbling a word to either SW or the officer, walking back to my dorm room a short distance away. I would return to the car a short time later with a couple of the Raeford gang and remove the remaining wine that was still sitting on the floorboard. Blue would make a comment to the effect that I had left the white boy hanging. I knew Blue's observation was right on target. Actually, I did not need for him to point that out to me; my guilty conscience began bothering me before I set foot out of the car.

I would see SW the next day and he would calmly relate the details of his arrest. He was actually released a couple of hours after getting to the station without being charged. I believe the police folks felt sorry for SW after finding out what a nice guy he was and realizing also that he really was not that drunk. It didn't take much for SW. I'm sure seeing his black buddy and drinking partner walk away from him, leaving him holding the bag, helped their decision. SW had a look in his eye that was a mixture of anger and disappointment. Though I would apologize for having left him, SW was not ready to let it go. I would crucify myself for years afterwards for not having been a true friend or more loyal companion that evening.

A short time after that situation, SW would be involved in a near fatal car crash and my guilt would magnify even more. I did manage to make myself go see him in the hospital, in spite of my guilt. SW would almost fully recover. He would recover enough to one afternoon nearly bite my thumb off during a physical altercation between us over what I knew was something minor. Both of us knew where his rage toward me really extended from. I intentionally did not harm him in defending myself. After that, we would go our separate ways – in our individual states of discomfort. I saw him very infrequently after that. I agreed with him; his continued anger at me was more than justified.

* * *

I entered St. Andrews Presbyterian College in September 1976 on both an athletic and academic scholarship. St. Andrews was a small private school with an enrollment of less than 500 students, compared to approximately 2,000 students at Wingate. With my vaunted 3.89 GPA I brought from Wingate and a preceding reputation of being a good runner, I was a BMOC (Big Man On Campus) the first day I arrived. Some of the other students already knew who I was: "a scholar and an athlete." I played the role to the hilt beginning almost immediately. My, how things had changed in a relatively short period of time after leaving Wingate with regard to my then vaunted ego. I was full of myself, enjoying the attention to the max. To cap everything, the campus housing department at St. Andrews had assigned me to a coed dorm. Though some anxiety existed with me being in such a situation, a bigger part of me was in "hog heaven. "My first evening there I would get an invitation to a party in the female suite next door. I drank a huge volume of liquor and wine, smoked a little marijuana, and ended up spending the night with the primary host of the gathering. Because of still remaining anxiety, my drunken stupor, and me really not being physically attracted to the young lady, I did not perform as a man should. Technically, my virginity was still intact. I would rise at five o'clock feeling a piece of garbage, not so much because of the drugging the night before, but more so because of my sexual performance. I proceeded on to morning cross country practice anyway. Needless to say, I was not very motivated that particular morning.

I would see B, the party host, later that day after classes outside the dorm inner courtyard and was surprised that she did not look at me with angry or condescending eyes. She spoke, with a half-smile on her face. Of course, I was not doing nearly as well. My disappointment in me the night before was gnawing at me immensely as I stood there chatting with her. I made up something to excuse myself from the uncomfortableness. I headed inside my suite to my room, shut the door and, leaving the lights off, stretched out across my bed with my eyes shut. That awful emotional pain came and it seemed that no amount of me trying to redirect my thoughts made any difference. After about 45 minutes I managed to rouse myself up enough to make evening practice. My motivational level had not improved at all. In fact, it seemed to have decreased.

* * *

It was there at St. Andrews that I picked up the nickname of Iceman, an upgrade from my Cool Curt moniker earned at Wingate. Folks used to say: "We don't see how you can walk around campus so slow, yet run so fast." My overall sober demeanor contributed to that personality assessment. I was generally quiet and calm; my shyness was evident. What was not so readily apparent to my newfound cohorts was my almost nonexistent in-depth social skills. I was afraid of people and just did not know how to act.

My alcohol consumption would increase and so would my recreational (other) drug use. Not only was I smoking marijuana, but also I was occasionally indulging in acid, cocaine, hash, Quaaludes, valium, speed and mushrooms. The drastic change in my personality, going from the "Iceman" to "Mr. Party" was especially noticeable there. With the campus being so small, it didn't take long for the word to get around, particularly talk surrounding my behavior when I was drunk and in blackouts.

For a while I worked in the Rec Room in the gym during the evenings, where I would from time to time "short" the cash register for money to buy cigarettes and wine. When inquires were made about all the money not being there, I would blame it on not having charged some of the folks the appropriate fees that particular evening. Usually, that excuse was accepted, though I would be admonished each time for having come up short. There would be two young local high school girls who would regularly frequent the campus and the Rec Room. They fondly referred to me as the devil man, because of my eyes they would say. I would smile and chat with them a while and go on to other things. Little did they know that each time they referred to me as the devil man, a piece of me believed that I actually was that bad.

The 3.89 GPA that I left Wingate with had reduced to 2.75 by the time I graduated from St. Andrews in May of 1978. As I moved from the darkness to the light with my alcohol and other drug consumption, and as I became more and more caught up in chasing love (and running from it at the same time), my focus -50- on academic matters dwindled. I eventually stopped putting forth much effort.

My need to be recognized in such a fashion became secondary. I simply did not care any more. I remember a couple of different people expressing disappointment with my academic performance based on the record that I had brought with me from Wingate. I was disappointed as well, but by then it was a moot issue. I floated between the emotional pain and the drugs and the desires of fulfillment from others. Social Security funds from my mother's death were even stopped after Uncle Sam inquired about my grades following my first semester at St. Andrews. The campus was more lax than Wingate. Partying was definitely more overt and more acceptable.

I am sure that I had some semblance of a nervous breakdown the last semester, even though I did not acknowledge it then. I did relatively well, as long as popular opinion about me was apparently positive. When the talk about me became more negative than positive, my psyche would again revisit the land of no confidence – over and over again. The panic attacks (of the social phobia type*) and my paranoid side became more prevalent, and there was seemingly no peace to be found. (* If two or more folks focused their attention entirely on me for any sustained period of time, I would begin shaking all over. The hot flashes would come, along with the occasional psychological threat of passing out.) I absolutely hated those times, not being able to control such a reaction. I hated me for not being mentally stronger.

The only peace I thought was available to me was the temporary solace created by the drink and/or the pill. Speaking of which, I found myself with more frequency combining the two chemicals, increasing the times during which I blacked out. I would awaken from one such blackout and find myself in the middle of the campus lake with a guy that I had been popping 747s (Quaaludes) and drinking liquor with on a paddle boat. Neither of us had on a life jacket. Once I realized where we were, I suggested we make our way back to shore. Another time I would awaken and find myself being assisted up from the steps of the outer gym complex by two student athletes. There was a gash in the back of my head where I had fallen backwards onto the concrete steps. I had sat down apparently after reaching the steps and then just keeled over backwards. It is my understanding that a host of peers walked past to view the sight before the two guys came by and made an effort to revive me. Not being able to remember going through the changes of both those situations only created more shame and guilt for me.

During this period of time, my mental state became more and more fragile.

A form of paranoia increased in prevalence with regards to the words of songs and the spoken words of individuals. Things got to the point that it did not matter whether I was under the influence or not, every song that I heard was directed at me! Those around me would note the change in me depending on the words of a particular song; the internalization would show on my face. One young lady on campus who had observed me on several occasions react to the music offered me counsel once, encouraging me with, "Curtis, they are not talking about you in the song; stop reacting to it; just enjoy the song." I knew when she made that statement to me that I was in pretty bad shape.

Others, who were aware of this tendency, would intentionally say something to get a reaction out of me. Oftentimes, I delivered. In fact, one such guy made reference to his having thought about becoming a homosexual and then intentionally moved closer to me. He was wearing only a towel, having just taken a shower – following soccer practice. I immediately tensed up and began to fidget and sweat. The guy, who was a transplant from Kenya (that seemed to make it worse for some reason) would then comment, "Man, your mind is weak!" He was absolutely correct. What would the boys have thought about such a reaction. They would have disowned me. He obviously had little or no respect for me.

Social relationships were a struggle for me. I could be somewhat affectionate when under the influence of drugs, but when sober, the ability to be that way was far removed. This became so apparent to others on the small campus that in a sociology class in January of 1978 when the subject of "love" was broached, a female student pleaded with the professor to allow everyone in class to give their definition of what love meant to them. After a Momentary pause and several eyes including the professor's turning in my direction, the petition was denied. My apparent reputation for being unemotional when sober was alive and well.

Most of the folks in that classroom had been aware of my relationship with a certain lady on campus during my freshman year. This lady, much older than I, was the individual with whom I had officially lost my virginity. The scenario played out was vintage me. By night and after a few drinks, I would be warm and loving toward her, and everything was good between us. By day, I did not have the whatever to be the same with her. This would hurt her badly on more than one occasion. She wanted to be acknowledged as being more than just a friend when we were in the public domain, as she had every right to desire. It had not been easy for her to give herself to me, particularly in a sexual way. A previous relationship had scarred her deeply and allowing herself to get to that level of trust with another man had been difficult. That previous relationship had ended with her seriously contemplating suicide. Many times I wished that it would have been someone else that she had chosen to revisit such emotional depths with. Many times I wished that I would seek her company when sober rather than having the ability to seemingly do that only when drinking. Looking from the outside, it appeared that I had used her just to satisfy my sexual and emotional needs, but in my heart, I knew that I was not that cold, selfish and cruel. I do not blame anyone for believing otherwise. After all, I was a man, one that had a great deal of difficulty exhibiting normal and appropriate emotions.

I would often get angry with myself for not being able to display those normal, social, emotional and physical interactive skills. I knew some people really did like me, but I didn't know how to accept it, simply because I didn't like me! And I really couldn't see at that time how anyone else could truly like me. I would catch myself when interacting with others at St. Andrews frequently asking them, "Ain't I good?" It finally dawned on me "why" I had developed a habit of tacking that question onto conversation pieces, particularly when the topic revolved around something I had done for someone else. I didn't believe I was good. For so many negative things to have happened to me, I must be a bad person! For seemingly having nobody to love me, I could not be a good person!

* * *

I went home for a weekend visit a couple of months prior to graduating from St. Andrews. As had been the pattern since leaving high school, I spent a great deal of time while there hanging out with the guys on the corner. As usual, we all drank wine, liquor and beer, as well as smoked dope. And per usual also, I ended up going into a blackout and acting the fool. Following my Saturday night performance, which I did not remember, my Uncle Will relayed to me the next day: "Boy, you are still as crazy as ever. Do you know you were down here last night drunk and trying to fight again. You kept saying over and over again, 'I ain't fought nobody here in Morven!' You broke my watch when I grabbed you to stop you." This blackout verbal barrage by me made me aware of just how messed up my psyche really was. A drunk man speaks what a sober man things, I guess. I still remember those words of Uncle Will as if he had spoken yesterday.

What eventually registered boldly in my mind was how I had been sucked up into the street culture of that little town; how subtly ingrained things I thought were a part of being cool and accepted, had crept into my brain without my being really conscious of them. I felt like a fool, standing there listening to Uncle Will tell me about the night before. But the guys, the few that I ran into back on the block that Sunday before going back to school, did not laugh or make fun this time. It was almost like they felt my pain for the first time and that they saw vividly what the code of street conduct had helped create and they literally felt sorry for me. Nearly all the times before then and numerous times after that, the guys' reaction had been and would be one of anger or one of chiding ridicule. I remember thinking during the ride back to St. Andrews that I shouldn't have gone home that weekend, rather than thinking something more like I'm screwed up inside emotionally and mentally and the drinking and the drugging are not helping.

* * *

I graduated from St. Andrews on a Saturday in May and left without saying good-bye to anyone. I did not linger after the ceremony and exchange addresses, hugs and kisses, as is the custom. I did everything but actually run - in leaving the institution, more out of shame and guilt than anything else. The bottle of Thunderbird wine, a graduation gift from one of my cousins, pacified me during the forty minute drive back to Morven. While I recognized that I had accomplished something no one else had ever done in my family – graduating from college – there was no real sense of accomplishment – because of the inner turmoil that raged within my soul.

While sitting in the back seat sipping on the bottle of wine, in between making chit-chat conversation, my mind would drift back to the beginning of that senior year at St. Andrews. Having come off a successful junior year in terms of athletics and the popularity

(No) Sex, Drugs and the Blues 65

thereof, my BMOC mentality was riding high. My false ego was in full stride. I had been All Conference in Cross County, MVP in Track and Field, and had lettered in basketball as well. I had set the school record in the 440 yard dash and had been given credit for providing the impetus for St. Andrews winning its first Cross Country and Track and Field Conference Championships back to back years. I was considered by some to potentially be an Olympic-caliber runner, if I would be able to get myself together and stop the self-destructive behavior.

I remembered times of depression during my initial track season when the monkey rode my back so hard, that I refused to go to one of the early meets. Obviously, my coach and teammates were disappointed in me. Some of the folk had assumed that I was fearful of facing one of the conference's other premier runners. Oh, how I wished that it had actually been that simple. How could I explain (in words) to those guys, the pain that was ripping at my insides. Some may have understood, others would not have really cared. I had let the team down. More poignantly, I had let me down, again.

I only played basketball my junior year. I just tried out because of the encouragement of Arthur B., a homeboy from Wadesboro, who was the acknowledged star of the team. Later the thought occurred to me that I would be able to say to folks, "I played college (basket) ball" in the years down the road. Besides starting for the JV team, I really saw very little action playing with the varsity squad. I traveled most of the road games, but rarely saw action, unless the score was heavily slanted one way or the other. Once, I even refused to enter a game when we were trailing by 20 plus points with less than a minute left to go. How bold could I have been? I'm sitting there thinking the couch should have put me into the game much sooner. I had Momentarily forgotten my penchant for freezing and becoming nearly incapacitated by the crowd when on the court.

I certainly never played up to my natural skill level.

During the preseason of that year, we had gone back to Bowman High School to play an intra-squad game. This was a yearly tradition; the two coaches, Thacker (Bowman High) and Whitely (St. Andrews) were friends. I remember being both proud and anxious to be going back to the high school where I had once suffered so much emotional pain and ridicule, as a member of a college basketball team.

Though I had played basketball in junior high, none of the high school coaches had ever given me a second look. Instead of pride making me strive to look presentable, physical appearance and otherwise, I intentionally did not undo the self-done nappy braids and comb my hair out. I made no attempt to remove the ash from the exposed parts of my body. Inside my pea brain head I was scoffing at my old acquaintances, saying, "Look at me now; I've got hair now; I'm on a college basketball team. You all can kiss my ass. I don't care what you think about me now." Of course, I did care. Only after we loaded up to head back to St. Andrews did I really realize just how angry my mindset had been. I wished I could go back and re-do the experience, but…

* * *

I would make the assumption that because of who I was on campus, I would probably have no problem scoring with any lady there. My first night back, hanging out in the University Center, I ran into P whom I had gotten to know fairly well during our junior year. She was a senior also. P and I would exchange pleasantries and I would ask to escort P back to her dorm room.

On the way I am thinking that I am not really physically attracted to this lady, but hey, I might as well go ahead and bed her, make her night, just because … Of course, I had no idea P would react like she did when I verbally posed the proposition to her. She was stunned and shocked, screaming at the top of her lungs, "Curtis, I just want to be your friend; I don't want to make love to you."

Others in the dorm at the time would hear her and come running to her rescue, not knowing if I was trying to force myself upon her or not. P would continue to cry hysterically after "help" arrived, a bit of an over reaction probably, but nevertheless, there it was …

The searing and convincing eyes of the crowd would pierce my soul as I tried to apologize to P. Feeling as if I had just committed the worst sin imaginable, I would hastily make my exit from the dorm. The next morning as I entered the cafeteria for breakfast, the judgmental eyes of everyone fell upon me. Word had already got around that I had tried to force myself on P. As I paused for a Moment, somewhat surprised by the condemnation, I knew that I would never be able to live it down. And I would not. I knew within myself that I would never force myself on P, or anyone else for that matter, drunk or sober, but many of my peers chose to believe otherwise. The critical eyes and the whispering would remain to some degree for the remainder of the school year. Only after that Fall semester would P verbally acknowledge me in passing with a subdued "hi". I would heap more punishment and condemnation upon myself than any of the others. My mentality of that fateful evening of being a BMOC having had whoever I wanted would stay with me forever. It would be years later before I would finally forgive myself.

In actuality, I spent a great deal of time at St. Andrews sexually frustrated, along with everything else. I would feel guilty for wanting it, I would feel less than a man for not having the ability to get there. No matter how many times the opportunities for some bedroom action were there, the overkill of the alcohol usually negated those Moments. It was a no-win situation. I had to have the alcohol or other type drug to establish the confidence in me to make such an approach. Of course, when I got there, I believed it was my duty to score. After all, I was from Morven, North Carolina. Besides the lady who was responsible for me officially losing my virginity, there was no other woman during my tenure at St. Andrews that I really wanted to sleep with. I wish my training had been of a different breed. I'm sure I missed out on some tremendous opportunities to get to know some of those folks. In any event, I don't think the boys would have been impressed with my results in this realm either.

4
Uncle Sam (Doesn't) Want Me

> *"There are times when we feel there is no way up or out. Illness. Poverty. Confusion. Loneliness. Desperation. They take us to a place called "rock bottom". In these times you may feel weak and vulnerable, and it is easy to lose faith in your ability to go on…"*
>
> — *Acts of Faith,* Iyanala Vanzant

After leaving St. Andrews, I made a half-hearted attempt to find a position in social services. I sent out only three resumes, getting zero responses, of course. Between hanging out on the street corner and getting lit, I interviewed for and got a job in a dye plant in Wadesboro, ten miles from Morven. The job lasted approximately six months before they fired me for poor attendance and for being under the influence a couple of times when there. With the loss of that job, hanging out on the corner became a full time occupation for the next several months. I bummed around like most of the other guys did; we would occasionally drink Alcorex, or rubbing alcohol, the preferred drink of several of the elder gentlemen in town, when funds were not sufficient enough to buy the real thing. We would generally mix about a fourth of a bottle with the same amount of water and drink it all down in one elbow bending exercise and pop into our mouths a piece of bubble gum to offset the bitter taste. Needless to say, its intoxicating effect was almost immediate and we would be good to go for at least a couple of hours.

As always, I was continually seeking legitimate acceptance

from the boys. There was a time when I graduated from Wingate that I frequented the local "hole-in-the-walls" or nightclubs. It was the thing to do. I had to be well on my way to being drunk to feel even half comfortable while there. I did not have the intestinal fortitude to simply refuse the requests to go to such places. But during those times following Wingate, there was little fear hanging out in them assuming I had my elixir, of course. Almost always there would be physical altercations, along with the occasional senseless shootings and knifings. Friend or foe, it did not seem to matter when it came to living up to that macho creed. Besides the alcohol, the biggest reason I felt so confident then was because of the positive publicity I had received during and after leaving Wingate. With my achievements there came a large measure of respect. I was liked! Sure.

* * *

My, what a difference a couple of years made in terms of that once temporary respect. After my freaking out episodes made news around the surrounding communities, along with my air of no fear and invincibility when drunk, the tide would turn. Through very little direct verbal assistance of my own, the word got around that I thought I was bad. With the folks no longer viewing me in such a positive light, I couldn't get drunk enough or high enough to feel comfortable in that environment. I would be challenged to fight by someone almost every time out. I would usually end up getting myself beaten. I lacked physical coordination when drunk; everything from busted lips and black eyes to a bruised neck and spine.

One specific incident that I recall with clarity is walking into a club one Saturday night with one of my cousins. All eyes immediately turned to me when I entered. My anxiety increased tenfold as the dude, BR, with the reputation of being the baddest fellow around approached me with a wry grin on his face and extended a hand in mock sincerity. I knew at that point what was going on. I paused for a Moment then shook his hand and looked around the dimly lit, smoke-filled room. My eyes stopped on my brother Paul's eyes as he stood there with the apparent same sense of anticipation and expectation as everyone else. The fear, anxiety, and hurt nearly overwhelmed me as I turned and walked out of the club. The folks had been waiting for my arrival. My cousin had seen to it that I made it there that night for the show. I failed to deliver. It was obvious to me as well that several of the other tough guys were waiting in line for an opportunity at me, just in case BR left something undone.

Paul would come outside a few Moments later and verbally and unmercifully express his disappointment with me. I was hurt by his disappointment with me. Feeling like the lowest thing on the face of the planet, I would hang around outside the club until one of the other boys was kind enough to give me a ride home. Paul had returned inside to try to bring some sense of honor back to the Wall name, I guess. I was never really able to live that night down, but the talk on the street did move on to other things after a few days.

* * *

Mr. Hall, a teacher at the high school stopped on the corner one afternoon several days after that incident and encouraged me to apply for an assistant teacher job. A couple of other people, including "sis," had earlier reminded me of my need to vacate that corner scene. The position Mr. Hall mentioned to me had been newly created to help the local secondary students pass the state proficiency test the second time around. I sobered up long enough to apply for and get the position. A couple of week earlier, I had also signed up for the National Guard. The decision to do such a thing had come by way of a radio advertisement and a vision. I was lying in bed recovering from a flare up of that inflamed gum disease and a major case of depression. I knew I was supposed to make that move to enlist. The flare up of my gums had provided me with a temporary excuse to stay off the corner for a while. After all, I truly did not want to be out there anyway. I welcomed almost any excuse to get away from it.

Though I had always held negative feelings about joining any branch of the armed services, most likely because of my penchant for authority figures – not liking anyone to tell me what to do – I really felt drawn to this path. It came over me about that same time to get my "Afro" cut off. Along with that occurrence came a new attitude about myself and the dreaded concern about my head and hair was gone. It was a good feeling! In fact, Snake, one of the homeboys would comment the afternoon I'd gotten my hair cut, "Curtis, you've been talking a whole lot more shit since you got your hair cut." And he was right. With the haircut came a certain release, a freedom, from no longer having to wear a hairstyle for the sake of being like everyone else. Perhaps I was on to something here.

By all accounts, I did well in working with the students in preparing them to retake the exam. In fact, nearly 90% of the kids that I worked with passed the test the next time around. I received a great deal of encouragement to go back to school and get my certification so that I could become a bona fide teacher at the school. I never chose to exercise that option. I gave the matter only semi-intensive thought, as I knew my lot rested some place else. I had no clear vision of exactly where, I just knew that it was not in the classroom as a full time teacher. Though I would have loved being in a position to make a difference in the lives of young people, the environment would have been too confining and too restrictive for me. As screwed up as my life was at that time, I knew that my spirit needed to soar in order to find true peace and contentment.

* * *

Shortly after going to work at the high school, I bought my first car, a tan Ford Pinto Runabout. I was 24 years old. I was warned about the car after I had picked it out by one of the boys who was with me. He said that everybody knew that the car had been owned by a girl in Lilesville, and that she had blown up the engine in the car several months earlier. I heard, but I didn't hear, the statement. The car was priced at $600.00 and was all I could afford. I took the deal. Even without the benefit of a valid driver's license, I convinced the used car dealership to allow me to work out the details for my tags and insurance. I had failed the driver's license test earlier, probably due to nervousness, anxiety and no confidence. I told them that this would be taken care of in a matter of the next several days after the purchase. I left the lot with a 20-day drive-out tag attached to the inside of my back window.

The Pinto was a five speed, straight shift, which I did not know how to drive. My partner would end up driving the car home for me. Over the next several days I learned how to shift gears and half-way handle the car. There was a 3-4 day delay in that learning experience because the gear shift had to be replaced; it had popped out the second day I had the car home. I recall folks always giving me plenty of room at the stoplight if they found themselves behind me. My driving ability, or lack of, became another source of ridicule from the boys. I knew that the primary reason I was having so much difficulty becoming accustomed to driving was because I so worried about what people were saying about me and my lack of driving proficiency. The boys would tolerate me in the vehicle, mainly because it beat the hell out of walking. I felt more relaxed and in control when drinking, but, of course, actually had less control at that point.

Everybody who knew me knew that I didn't have a driver's license, nor did I have insurance on the car. The twenty-day grace period would come and go; I would not have made any effort to secure either. I would embarrass myself more than once. In a semi-drunken stupor I would run the car to the edge of an embankment before being able to stop it. The car's front wheels actually hung over the edge of the ravine, which appeared to be 15-20 yards steep at a 70-degree angle. Since we could not push or pull the car back and away from the edge, one of the boys would end up getting behind the wheel and driving the car down into, through, and out of the ravine. It had not rained for several days, and a visual inspection of the terrain yielded that it may be feasible to just drive the Pinto down and through the ravine. It worked. We pushed the car from behind as it rolled quickly down the embankment.

On our way to a Saturday afternoon community baseball game,

I would nearly blow the engine in the Pinto myself by downshifting from 5 to 3 going at approximately 50 miles an hour. The guys in the car with me looked at one another and silently snickered when the car jolted and backfired. Of course, minutes after arriving at the ball field, everyone knew about the incident. After about 45 minutes of tolerating the abuse (and sipping Smirnoff) I decided to leave the jeering eyes and comments. I would scrape my cousin's car as I tried to maneuver my way through the dirt and dusty parking lot maze. Naturally, he was upset, but feeling pity for me, he let the situation go with a semi-warning to my brother Paul that he needed to make sure I got away from there in short order. Even though the damage to my cousin's car was minimal, had it been someone's car not related to me and someone having no compassion, I surely would have gotten a good old fashioned butt-whipping that afternoon.

Three or four days later I would find myself drunk again and driving my Ford Pinto, with four other lost souls, around a curve at a high rate of speed. I was not able to bring the Pinto out of the curve on schedule. The car would flip at least once before coming to rest upside down. Fortunately, none of us were seriously injured. A couple of the guys had fairly deep lacerations, but that was about it. There were no broken bones or severe cuts and bruises. I did not have a scratch on me. We were all transported to the hospital for observation and released the same evening. Whew!...and only by the Grace of God. The car had been totaled. Since I had no insurance, my brief era with the Pinto Runabout came to an end. I would sell the car several days later to a local mechanic for a couple of hundred dollars.

There were no formal charges filed by law enforcement, perhaps another small miracle. Sheriff's deputies did come by my house a couple of times to question me; both times I was either at work or track practice (coaching). The fear of my being arrested and charged became so intense that I intentionally walked approximately four miles of the 13 mile trek home one day before accepting a ride from someone. The four-mile hike was essentially through the town of Wadesboro, the county seat, where the sheriff's deputies were stationed. I would pass three different patrol cars;

one would even slow down to get a closer look at me. I felt he recognized me. The point I was attempting to make was that I was not hiding from them; this time, I was not hiding from the consequences of my actions. They never came looking for me after that day. In any event, I was able to complete my tenure as an assistant teacher and track coach. I would catch a ride with Mr. Hall to work and hitchhike home. In that regard, nothing much had changed since my own high school days. My insane consumption of alcohol would continue.

* * *

I was scheduled to undergo basic training at Fort Leonardwood, Missouri, in June of 1979. The night prior to my leaving held some significant factors. It turned out to be my first formal attempt at suicide. I had consumed maybe a pint of liquor that evening when I attempted to see my girlfriend, who I had met while working at the high school. She was employed at one of the local manufacturing plants while awaiting college entrance in the Fall. Her supervisor refused to allow her to take a break at the time of my arrival, so I proceeded to drink some more with the boys and ended up going home around 11:30 p.m. I remember hurting emotionally, more so than usual. I didn't want to go off to basic training the next day; I was just tired – of everything. It would be several years before I would come to realize a startling truth; I did not really want to die that night, it was the emotional pain that I was seeking relief from.

I got an 8 oz. glass, filled it with Clorox, added approximately 3 oz. of rat poison, stirred the mixture and turned it up, swallowing the entire contents. I laid down in my little fold-away bed, shut my eyes, crying ever so gently and quietly. I was supposed to get up the next morning at 5:00 a.m. to get to Charlotte and catch my flight to Missouri. Obviously, I did not bother to set an alarm clock. I felt no physical discomfort as I drifted off to sleep. I awoke the next morning at exactly 5:00 a.m., with (still) no discomfort or side-effects from the concoction consumed the night before. I was upset that I was still alive; I was in awe that I was still in the world. I got up and proceeded off to Charlotte to catch my flight. On the plane, I thought about the events of the night before, how miserable I still felt, and how much I was dreading basic training. With the passage of time, during my healing process, I would realize just how miraculous that night truly was.

About a week before that I had experienced my first alcoholic delusion.

Sada Thompson of the television show, Family, was doing what I believe was a public service announcement. On that particular evening she was talking only to me. It seemed very real as she drew me closer to the television screen, as if to say, I don't want you to miss anything I am saying. I remember being awed by the experience and thinking how nice she was to stop acting long enough to talk to me. The test of her message remains unclear. That delusion would prove to be one of several that would follow as my drinking continued.

* * *

Ain't no need in going home, Jody's got your girl and gone; Am I right or wrong; are we going strong; sound of.......

We were confined to base the first three weeks of basic training. When Friday of the end of the third week rolled around, we were informed that we would be allowed to leave the base that evening to have some fun – if we chose. Because of my college degree, I was allowed to wear PFG bars on my collars. All but three other recruits had to wear the standard Private bars. I had already been approached about Officer's Candidate School as well. On this particular Friday evening, I remember being impressed with how good I looked. My false ego was riding high again. Not only was I one of only four out of more than 80 folks in my company to sport the PFC bars, but I also wore a super jock patch on my left sleeve and a squad leader band on my right. I was too full of me.

Along with several other guys from my squad, I headed straight for one of the local bars on base. I remember walking in the front door and being almost immediately approached by three female recruits already in the bar. They were obviously impressed with me also. I chatted with them for a few minutes and then proceeded upstairs to commence with my primary purpose for being there – to get drunk!

There was an exotic dancer doing her thing on a raised platform when I walked into the upstairs room. Donna Summer's 1979 hit "Bad Girl" still rings in my mind, as it was the feature song of the evening. The young lady dancing seemed to express herself more provocatively whenever that particular song came on. I had taken a table toward the back of the room and settled in drinking my favored Smirnoff Vodka, 90 Proof – straight, without a chaser or mixer. I do not remember a lot of interaction with other folks there; I mostly sat and drank, watching the dance routines while enjoying the music. After several drinks I set my half-empty glass of Vodka on the table and went downstairs to use the bathroom. I went back upstairs, sat down and finished the rest of my drink, without thinking anything about anything.

The next thing I knew – I was back at my company, with handcuffs being removed from my wrists. I remember the flashing lights from the Military Police vehicles. At that point I drifted back into another blackout. According to the guys in my unit, I passed out; my heart stopped beating. One of the guys reportedly then performed CPR and mouth-to-mouth resuscitation to revive me. I do recall later waking in the hospital and struggling with hospital staff who were trying to draw a blood sample to determine a possible drug overdose. I fought the staff so vehemently they were not able to obtain the sample. I was released from the hospital the next day. I had definitely lost the respect of some of my squad members, as well as my drill sergeants. This was mostly noted by a drastic change in attitude toward me. A couple of the guys helped me piece together what had likely happened that evening.

Upon leaving my drink on the table while going downstairs to use the bathroom, someone slipped a "mickey" in the drink, a dissolvable drug. I was told by other folks who were there that a short while after finishing the drink I was approached by three marine recruits. They were surmised to be the "boyfriends" or "dates" of the three female recruits who had approached me when I first entered the bar. Per eyewitness accounts, a fight ensued shortly after the marines accosted me and the MPs were called. Supposedly, I was doing a pretty decent job defending myself.

We were allowed to leave the barracks the next weekend. I made it a point to visit the same bar, around the same time as I had the previous weekend. I again went upstairs, bought a drink and sat down at the same table as before. I watched as people entered the upstairs area, wanting to see if somehow I recognized the marine recruits. I had not been aware otherwise of what was going on around me in the meantime, but I would glance around behind me and there was a line of fellow "soldiers" sitting behind me. One of them leaned forward and said, "Let us know if you recognize those guys from last week." I had done little talking about my primary purpose for being there, but word had gotten around in the bar that I was upstairs again, sitting and watching. Several of the trainees sitting behind me I did not even know; a couple of them were not even in my company. That made me feel pretty good. Nothing happened, as the marine recruits did not show up, at least not during the three to four hours I was there.

In spite of the support shown me by some of the guys during my return trip to the club, again I had lost a lot of respect from many of the other guys in my company. Because of my age and college degree, many of them looked up to me. Being so irresponsible though, with my drinking and trusting people in that bar setting said loud and clear that I was not quite as mature as my otherwise sober and quiet demeanor indicated. As one of the fellows said to me on Monday morning following the weekend episode, "You ain't cool anymore." He was one of those other guys with the PFC bars on his collar, and he was absolutely correct in his analysis. Actually, I wasn't really cool before that, in spite of my false sense of bravado on Friday evening. I could tell also that the drill sergeants saw me in a different light. Most of the folks did not know what to think about me. I was never able to live the experience down. "See ya round, crazy man," was what another of the recruits said to me on graduation day, as we were all departing to our individual corners of the military world.

* * *

I managed to complete basic training without any more significant episodes of disruption or problems created by my drinking and emotional immaturity. Another vision a couple of weeks prior to completing basic training moved me to commit to Active Duty (Regular Army) rather than maintain my National Guard status. I returned home for a brief period and then headed off to Fort Campbell, Kentucky to begin my three year tour of Active Duty. Upon arrival at Fort Campbell as a PFC, I was slated to be promoted to Spec 4 after four months and then head off to OCS two months after that. It did not take the folks long at Fort Campbell to realize that I was not officer material.

My heavy consumption of alcohol and the resulting embarrassing episodes of behavior saw to that. I did my best to hide the fact that I did not have a driver's license, including driving other guys' vehicles. In fact, one of the sergeants in the company regularly offered me use of his car. It was not so much that he was such a great guy, he called himself getting in good with someone who may eventually be his superior officer one day. He could have and probably would have taken more advantage of that situation, except for the fact, that my insecurity about driving a car when not having the false courage stimulated by the alcohol was always a potent force. Every now and then it would dawn on me that I was a 23-24 year old "man" going through those type changes. I was supposed to be grown, but actually came nowhere near it spiritually, emotionally, and mentally.

My reputation as a drunk, as someone crazy, appeared to spread overnight.

The respect that I had been initially approached with upon my arrival there dwindled bit by bit, day by day. I became known as someone who could not get along with his fellow recruits, which was the result of arguments and occasional physical confrontations that came about after getting drunk. I often found myself being jealous of several of the other guys, because they were generally more accepted than I was. They were better socially than I was or they had other things (girlfriend, money, car, etc.) that I desired. The anger from days of old continued to burn within me as well. The macho man was definitely in effect; I failed, according to those who knew me, to meet that qualification. No surprise.

There were guys in my company who were obviously jealous of me and my position of pending promotion and officer school. They laid in wait for every mistake I made – to criticize my fitness to be an officer. Unfortunately, I gave them plenty of material to work with. Drinking to take away that awful loneliness I felt was a daily thing when we were not in the field. My fears and insecurities also seemed to grow in leaps and bounds. The boys had the old macho stuff to come at me with: hadn't had any (sex) since I'd been there. Here I go again; I simply could not escape that manly expectation. I would drown myself in the booze even more when those comments were dropped on me. Being in a drunken stupor also meant that I didn't have to deal with the natural physical urges of sexual gratification.

Several of the older guys had tried to steer me in the right direction. They initially offered encouragement and support. Those things were eventually nixed when they saw me making very little effort to help myself. After such things as me urinating in the hallway outside the bathroom one night when drunk and in a blackout, partially defecating once in my pants another time when drunk (yes, extensive alcohol overkill can actually get you there – the making of the wet brain syndrome), and crying hysterically at another Moment, of course when intoxicated, their supportive attitude toward me changed. Those were probably the most embarrassing situations my drinking had put me in. I was not a soldier; I was not a man. I knew I was a serious disappointment to them. Since I did not have any recollection of those things, it was easy for me to adamantly deny they ever had occurred. Surely, they got me confused with someone else. It was so easy at times to see my military career unfold, as it should. The rank, the respect, the discipline, the pride were all a part of that fleeting vision. So much of me wanted those things to come about. My bruised psyche had control, however. It ran the show the way it wanted to. I simply took what I was handed and never thought too often that I could actually change or control what was happening with me inside.

A 17 year-old white kid who had dropped out of high school had attached himself to me upon his arrival to the company a couple of months after I had made it there. Knowing that we were both relatively new and my showing some signs of having it together (when sober) made the attachment easy. Some of the other white guys though snatched him out of his tendency of hanging around me. They helped JW get his driver's license, in addition to taking him on a virginity-losing weekend adventure in Nashville. JW did not relate to me the same after those things, particularly the weekend in Nashville. In fact, he became one of my harshest critics, engaging in the mocking and sarcasm with regularity. I was disappointed in him. Did I blame him? No. He had slid into his little niche that was going to see him through his military experience. He became one of the (white) boys.

* * *

Friday, February 15, 1980, rolled around; I was scheduled to receive my Spec 4 promotion Monday, in spite of the in-house reputation that I had acquired since joining Fort Campbell's ranks. Friday was payday and the day after Valentine's, the day of love; I will never forget it. Though I proudly displayed an 8 x 10 photo of my Carolina girlfriend, my heart longed for close and/or sexual female companionship. At the same time, I was scared to death of such a possibility. I eventually stopped communicating with my girlfriend. The guys that had gotten to know me halfway knew that something was amiss, no matter how hard I gave the impression that true love was in the mix.

Everyone was looking forward to the weekend. Three of the guys from my company and I headed for "Hop Town" (Hopkinsville, Ky.), in the opposite direction of Clarksville, Tennessee. We got a bottle of liquor on the way and ended up stopping at one of the local pool halls downtown. We drank, shot pool and played cards. We met a guy named Freddie who was obliged to hang out with us. After 3-4 hours, the other guys decided to return to post; I decided I was going to party a little while longer with Freddie. Freddie and I left the pool hall, went by an ABC store, stopped at Wendy's for some food, and ended up at an apartment in the hood where a party was going on. I sat on the couch sipping my vodka straight, content and listening to the music from the stereo. Always when I got half lit from alcohol (or other drugs), the music would seem to sound much better, penetrating every fiber of my soul.

    A lady who appeared to be the hostess made it a point to ask me several times if I wanted a chaser for my drink; I would politely refuse each time. Finally after continuous badgering from her, I accepted her offer to get me a chaser – just to appease her. She and some guy went into the kitchen, came back a couple of minutes later and handed me a glass of water. I took a shot of vodka and chased it with the water.

    The next thing I knew, I woke up in the back seat of a blue station wagon. It was raining heavily. Freddie was in the front passenger seat, and a big dude with a beard and a navy blue toboggan was in the driver's seat. The car stopped along a dirt road. Both Freddie and the dude got out of the car and came to their respective sides of the car and opened the back doors where I was. Both guys reached in and grabbed everything I had on me that was of any value, money, watch, wallet, etc. I was well aware of what was happening, but I could not move. Freddie grabbed me by the collar, pulled me from the car and slung me into the nearby ditch. They got into the car and drove away.

    I slumped back into another blackout. A State Trooper stated that he normally did not come down that isolated road, but something told him on that particular morning to do so. He went on to say that it was around 2:00 a.m. in the morning when he came upon me. I was walking down the side of the road, soaking wet and covered with mud. Reportedly, he took me to the hospital on Post, where eventually a blood test was done: PCP overdose. When they had gone into the kitchen to get me a glass of water to chase my vodka, the girl and the dude had apparently put PCP in the water, which dissolved leaving no visible trace of its presence. I had been set up. I had been at the wrong place at the wrong time. I had been drunk.

    I woke up in the hospital with what seemed to be a tremendous erection.

    There was a nurse sitting beside my bed and I would plead with her to climb into bed and make love to me. She was a black lady who appeared to be in her late 30s or early 40s who would simply look at me with eyes of sadness and pity, while not responding to my request. I remember tears running down the side of my face as we Momentarily made eye contact. I would notice tears beginning to form in her eyes as well. Even with my clouded mental condition, I could tell that she did not have the heart to verbalize no to my sexual plea. But there was no mistaking that her answer was no. I could literally feel the compassion she had for me. I would apparently pass out again. She would not be there when I awoke later that day. I do not remember her name, but I hope one day to somehow have the opportunity to thank her for that Moment and to apologize.

    I would stay in the hospital for several days, thereby negating my promotion on Monday morning. In fact, nothing else would ever be said about the promotion. I returned to my company about mid-week to a rather subdued reaction from my fellow company members. My emotional state was in complete turmoil; my heart ached with more vengeance than it seemed liked it ever had before. My heart felt as if someone was taking a foot long needle and slowly pushing it in. But I made it to that weekend and hit the Top Six, a nightclub on base. Upon my arrival at Fort Campbell, the club scene had again become a fixture for me. In addition to meeting the new boys' expectations, I was more actively searching for female companionship as well. Anyway, I was drunk inside of an hour after getting there. One of the guys lent me some money. As far as I know, I got by that night with irritating only a few people. I had a well-developed habit of rubbing up folk, particularly females, the wrong way when drunk.

    Initially, because of flashback concerns from the PCP overdose,

I was not allowed to participate in field exercises nor allowed around explosives. I am not sure of the order of events that brought the military to the point of extending a choice for me to either "leave without being Dishonorably Discharged or stay and accept the consequences of my irrational behaviors." I do know that I ended up being placed on restriction, confined to my room at night after meal, and being threatened with legal action from writing bad checks. I was also disciplined for not being able to get along with fellow mates. That particular thing would soon lead me to being hospitalized again, this time in the psychiatric ward for an approximate two-week period. I would start fights when drunk with guys simply out of the same petty jealously mold of old: their popularity and acceptance. I would be ordered to attend counseling sessions on post. The couple of times I did make the appointments, I would walk the nearly eight-mile round trip trek.

No one offered me use of their car. I was too embarrassed by then to approach anyone to ask for a ride.

* * *

A couple days after my being released from the hospital again and placed on barracks restriction, I would be caught by the night CO with a bottle of liquor in my room. One of the guys, after my begging and pleading with him had consented to go to the liquor store for me and purchase a fifth of vodka. I had neglected to lock my door while sipping on the juice. The CO, making his regular rounds, would check my door, find it unlocked, open it, and spot the liquor bottle, still half-full, sitting on the floor next to my bed. He would take the bottle with him as he left. It was illegal to have alcohol in the barracks area. I would drift off to sleep.

Waking up the next morning and realizing that I was headed for another visit to my company CO on Monday morning, I freaked out. I decided to feign a suicide attempt. I broke the 8 x 10 picture of my girlfriend, creating enough noise so the folks in the hallway would hear me. I cupped pieces of the glass in both hands, while not responding to anyone's attempt to communicate with me as they entered the room. I was carried back down to the psychiatric ward again. This time the paperwork process to have me removed from the service was begun. The option was presented to me again and I decided that it was time for Uncle Sam and me to part ways. I completed the remainder of my stay until my ETS date, from the psychiatric ward.

    My final days at the hospital would be increasingly filled with more paranoia. The folks on the psychiatric ward were oftentimes laughed at and ridiculed for being on Ward 7. It became almost impossible for me not to react to the chiding of the hospital military staff. Saturday Night Live did a skit on the show back in those days featuring Mr. Bill. Mr. Bill was always getting hit, crushed, run over, or something else devastating. Mr. Bill's storyteller's condescending and irritatingly shrill voice was a critical part of the act. There would almost always be several of the fellow soldier boys assigned to the hospital that would walk past me and another patient and imitate the Mr. Bill voice. At that particular time, I could not help but react to it. Naturally, the mocking continued as long as I responded to it. At the same time, I resented like hell, me, for having put myself in a position where I was being mocked by others. After all, I was once considered to be "officer material. "And I would fall in love and be rejected at least four times while awaiting my exit date. Looking for love in all the wrong places… looking for love anywhere. I knew at that time that I simply wanted a woman to love (someone of my choosing, of course) and a woman to love me. By now, I was more than willing to settle for a relationship with someone on a lesser emotional level. My reputation and antics when under the influence had long since preceded me. There was a time when a female patient and I had planned to go AWOL – from the hospital and take our chances of surviving in the real world. Obviously, such a scheme had been concocted by two emotionally distraught individuals, searching and grasping for acceptance…for love…for true self. This young lady's attitude toward me suddenly changed after she was visited by a couple of her company buddies. It was immediately clear to me that those buddies had warned the lady about her new found friend. She refused to speak to me after that visit from her friends. I was hurt.

Later, I would think about the insanity of planning such a thing as going AWOL. Neither one of us had any serious money, we were both emotional cripples, and had very bad drug using habits. Emotional pain, not necessarily any type of psychological dysfunction, has tremendous power to misrepresent one's reality. Such was mine at that time.

* * *

My grandmother would pass away around April of that year, while I was still awaiting formal discharge from the service. The Red Cross would make the necessary arrangements for me to return to Morven to attend her funeral, only the second one I had attended in my lifetime. The funeral scene did not set well with me. I believe that such a disposition goes all the way back to Mom and (maybe even my grandfather). In any event, I did make it. I had a tremendous hangover from the night before that was simply unrelenting. An older male cousin let me know that they had to carry me into the house the night before like a little baby because I had passed out from the liquor.

I would not, however, accompany the burial procession to the cemetery. I walked back home (a short distance) following the funeral service at church.

Most of us proceeded to get drunk at that point. I did manage to walk up and view Grandma's body during the service. She had a peaceful look about her. Someone had remarked earlier upon my arrival home that she had talked about how proud she was of me before she died. I reacted with mixed emotions when I heard that. I had managed to keep my military troubles to myself, mostly out of shame and fear of ridicule. I was glad, though, that Grandma died with positive thoughts about me. That had not always been the case.

There were times before I left for basic training when I would get intoxicated and the old pains would come back to haunt me. I would find that land of out-of-control – Larry would rush home and actually tie me down with straps and sheets to keep me from hurting myself and/or someone else. This occurred several times. Of course, an 80-something grandmother did not need to be exposed to such outrageous behavior. I would return to Fort Campbell a couple of days after the funeral without having shared with anyone about what was happening with me there. I wanted to get by without them finding out for as long as I possibly could.

Back at Fort Campbell, I would come to deeply resent authority even more, being told to do anything by anyone. Only a small part of me still cared about the ongoing humiliation I was putting myself through. I hated being called "crazy" and "weird," but was seemingly unable to stop the actions that continually added to such a perception. I was at the point then, where I would go off to myself sometimes and cry, without being drunk. I wanted love and acceptance so badly, but they appeared far removed from my grasp. To cap everything off, I was so ensconced in the self-pity mold that I could see no light at the end of the tunnel, only one continuous stream of darkness. On June 8, 1980, Uncle Sam and I parted ways for the final time. I would end my tour of duty with a General Discharge (Under Honorable Conditions).

5
A Geographical Cure

> *Many folk either consciously or unconsciously have sought to cure their ill fortunes, perceived bad luck, or circumstances in life by seeking a change of venue. Many folk have likewise learned that they have taken the real problem along with them when the move was made. The real problem dwells within. We cannot run; we cannot hide from ourselves. Good, bad, or ugly, I am a constant with me always.*
>
> — CDW

On the bus ride to Nashville where I was to catch my flight to Morven, thoughts of failure and returning to the corner raced through my mind. A feeling of dread accompanied the thoughts each time they re-entered my brain after a brief hiatus. Though I did not acknowledge it on a surface level, I was again saying that I had no control over which direction my life took. The bus ride to Nashville seemed to take forever.

I had approximately three hundred dollars cash and my plane ticket already in hand. In an effort to delay, I'm sure, I decided to change my flight to the next morning rather than that evening. In the meantime, I would spend the night in a motel down on James Robertson Parkway that I had visited once. After checking into the motel, my next stop was at a nearby liquor store. Of course, I purchased Smirnoff Vodka (a pint). About half the pint was gone when I decided to call a lady of the evening; I had acquired the number on my previous trip there while still at Fort Campbell.

Business was apparently brisk that evening, because I was not able to get someone to come to my room until about 2:00 a.m.

I vaguely remember the young lady showing up. I have no recollection of what we did. I have no recollection of her leaving.

Around 6:00 a.m., there was a knock at my door that awakened me. I stumbled to the door, opened it, and there stood another young lady. She immediately made the comment, "I've heard about you; how much money do you have?" I went back and got my wallet off the nightstand. As I walked back to the door where the woman was waiting, I remarked to her that I only had $6.00 left. She quickly agreed to do it for that and we did. She would take my last $6.00 and leave. It would then dawn on me when this lady left that I was now broke.

There was no money to pay for the hotel room; there was no money for cab fare to the airport. I took a swig of vodka and contemplated what I was going to do. One thing for sure, I couldn't go back to North Carolina and the boys on the corner with no money. After a couple more swallows of the vodka, I decided the best thing to do would be to kill myself, but…not really. As time climbed on to mid-morning, the plan slowly came together. I knew check-out time was eleven o'clock. I figured that if I had not complied by then or shortly after, that someone would come to find me.

I got a razor blade from my shaving kit, laid towels on the floor next to the bed (I was so thoughtful, wasn't I?). I didn't want my blood to mess up the motel room floor. I proceeded to do mostly superficial slashes on my left forearm and wrist. I hung my arm off the side of the bed over the towel, as the blood began to stream down. With my right hand I grabbed the liquor bottle and took another shot of vodka. Then I waited.

At approximately 11:05 a.m., there was a knock at the door; I did not respond to it. About five minutes later there was a knock again; I still did not respond. A few seconds later I heard keys rattling; the door opened; a housekeeper stuck her head through the door. She let out a scream as she observed me lying half off the bed, with a pool of blood on the toweled floor. I pretended to be unconscious; the housekeeper ran down the walk to get help. A few minutes later a paramedic unit shows up, along with the Metro Nashville Police. While still pretending to be unconscious, I feel them pull me from the bed, lay me on my back on the floor and check my pulse. Someone shakes my body in some form or fashion. One of the guys says, "He's not coming around; he's not coming around!" Then one of them adds, "Break out the smelling salts." When I hear this I immediately hold my breath (I'm so brilliant, aren't I?). When I do not respond to the salts, one of them suggests that they get me to Nashville General (Hospital) ASAP.

By the time we had arrived at Nashville General, I had slowly come around, still play-acting, of course. My eyes were open, but I was refusing to talk to anyone. After my refusing to answer numerous simple questions, one of the female nurses finally asked me if I would write a response. I nodded my head indicating yes. She then proceeded to ask, "Do you know anyone here in Nashville?" I took a pad and pen from her and wrote in response: "Yes, Conway Twitty, Loretta Lynn, and Charlie Pride." The nurse took the pad from me and looked at the response. She then read it aloud, looked at the other staff in the room and said: "This man is crazy: I suggest we ship him to the VA Hospital in Murfreesboro. Another staff person (a guy) posed a follow-up question to me. I do not remember the question. I hesitated, and before I could respond in any fashion, the female nurse snatched the pen from my hand and said, "Forget it! Let's just get him out of here." Almost immediately, the "Nurse Ratchet" from the movie, "One Flew Over The Cuckoo's Nest" popped into my head, as I glared at her while they wheeled me from the room. The male staff member apologized to me for her, but I knew that I should be the one extending an apology to them.

* * *

Less than an hour later, the ambulance pulled into the VA Hospital in Murfreesboro. The only thing I remember about that first evening is that a nurse asked me how often did I drink. I remember thinking: "Now, where would she get that from?" But it was not until that Moment that I actually thought out loud in my brain that I may, indeed, have a drinking problem. The thought was a fleeting one, however. Not since that little voice suggested to me following that first drink had I acknowledged this within me, brief or otherwise. Somewhere along the way, I had heard that as long as I boasted about my drinking, then I probably did not have a serious problem with it. How wrong that assertion had already proven to be.

 My stay at the hospital lasted approximately three and a half months. After probably a month I began to sneak off on Saturday afternoons, along with two or three other patients, to a local mart less than half a mile away. We would purchase beer or malt liquor with our monies pooled together. We would get as drunk as we could on what we had. Occasionally, someone would have marijuana. A couple of times I even huffed gasoline and sniffed glue, when there was not enough money to buy beer to get a good buzz. On one occasion, I was so drunk when I returned to my hospital ward that I passed out in the unit dayroom. Later the same evening I was awakened by one of the nurse aides, whom I had gotten to know, and was gently admonished for my afternoon behavior. I would eventually end up moving in with this lady, NNU, and her teenage daughter upon leaving the hospital several weeks later.

 The ward and hospital politics astonished me at times. My view of the world was still, apparently, very limited. I allowed staff and fellow patients to disappoint me time and time again. The most disheartening thing being there was watching the cruelty with which some staff members stabbed others in the back. From some of the doctors on down to the nurse aides, everyone sought to protect and feed their fragile egos. Everyone seemed to want to one-up everyone else. In the meantime, the patients were not receiving the quality care possible due to the personal staff battles going on. Of course some of the staff, particularly several of the nurse aides, really lorded themselves over us lowly patients. If, as a patient, staff in general took a liking to you, you could get away with pretty much anything you wanted to. If, on the other hand, the opposite turned out to be your luck, you often had hell to pay, in terms of being occasionally embarrassed and held to the letter of the law.

Some of those patients held in favor by majority staff were allowed to "run" their particular unit area during their stay. This sounds like a modified version of the prison scenario, huh? Those of us who resisted the control of the staff pets, were at times treated in an unprofessional manner by select staff members. I could not get with the program at all. As poorly as I felt about myself, I was not about to allow other folk as messed up as I was to dominate me. It simply was not going to happen. One female patient, in particular, who was supported by her first lieutenant, a bogus-assed white boy who spent the majority of his time split between kissing her behind and the rest of it kissing the butt of select staff, sought constantly to have some measure of control on our unit. I would have to hurt both of their feelings on more than one occasion.

The patient problems ranged from drug abuse and addiction to PTSD to true psychoticism. There would be occasional flare-ups between us that were laced with racial overtones. The black folks usually got pounced on harder by select staff. I don't know why I should have been so surprised about such happenings since the race issue has always been such a black-eye on the face of this potentially great nation.

When not involved with treatment-related activities, I began to write a great deal. I would write a song about "longing for love," send it off to Nashville, along with a borrowed $20.00, to have it recorded. The song was, in fact, recorded by singer/actor Ed Ames of the Old Daniel Boone TV series. I was not impressed. Obviously, the folks did just enough to fulfill their part of the agreement. At that time though, the effort made me feel better about me. I would end up getting a short story published in *Veterans' Voices* and in the publication, *Authors To Watch*. I knew that none of this was really a big deal in terms of me drawing attention to my writing ability in a huge way, but, the experience did my soul good.

I though back to that 9th grade high school experience where I was singled out by my English teacher for having done an exceptional job with an assigned composition. In fact, Mrs. Thomas would say some very kind words about the effort before reading it aloud to the class. The piece was entitled, "My Friend". It was a short expose about how I often depended on Jesus to help me make it through life on a daily basis. Obviously, though the anger was prevalent with the Spirit back then because of all the emotional pain and bad times, my true inner gut knew the real deal. And I was grateful.

Having always been fascinated by musical instruments, I would take advantage of the opportunity to take guitar lessons while at the hospital. The young lady teaching the class was the spittin' image of the country music legend, Barbara Mandrell, whose music I had occasionally gotten into. It was a difficult process trying to understand the finger placements on the instrument to create credible sound. The process itself was complicated more because of my heart palpitating for this girl. Here I go again, falling in love, looking for love, running from love. The young lady apparently sensed my yearning for her, because after a week, my therapeutic schedule was changed, and I was not allowed to return to the music department. I do not recall saying anything to her out of the way, or doing anything inappropriate; but for her to ask that I not continue with the guitar lessons, I must have been overflowing pretty badly. Inside, I knew that the girl was calling herself protecting me from getting hurt eventually by her having to nix my budding emotions. In fact, she was a very nice lady who obviously enjoyed helping others. I wish I would have been emotionally healthy enough to have been able to hang around her long enough to soak up some of her magic.

* * *

A black Chaplain at the hospital seemed to take a liking to me. In the beginning, the positive attention from him felt good. On the surface, his initial efforts toward me actually appeared to be genuine. Here was a black man, my brother, actually being willing to go out of his way to help me. He offered to find me a job and a place to stay upon my discharge from the hospital. A couple of weeks before my projected discharge, he took me to meet my prospective employer and my living quarters. My intended living quarters turned out to be the back of a long haul transport truck that was no longer in running condition. There were clothes and trash scattered everywhere, left by the previous tenant. Not that I was in any position to be choosy at that point about much of anything, but I was stunned by the proposed place of abode because the Chaplain had made such a big deal about having come through for me. I took the job, putting in telephone booth concrete poles, but would opt for other living arrangements.

The Chaplain wanted me to write a letter to the hospital administration expressing my gratitude for his efforts to help me. With that request, came the light bulb on in me regarding this dude. He had not done anything for me, rather everything had been done for himself, to make himself look good. I was angry; I was hurt. I refused to write the letter. He had very little to do with me after that point during my remaining time at the hospital. That was okay with me. As much as I desired attention from folks, I was not bothered by this particular separation. NNU would come to the rescue in terms of offering me her place to set up shop and making sure that I had transportation to the job, after my being discharged from the hospital.

It was not long after exiting the hospital that I submerged myself again into the street world/party scene. Nothing had changed since leaving Fort Campbell.

I embarrassed myself and NNU with my drunken behavior – at every turn. In between times, I sold vacuum cleaners for a while; I would get drunk one day on the job and quit later on the same afternoon – before being fired. I would also dabble in some tar roofing. I finally got a driver's license – at age 26! NNU and I would end up going to visit my folks in Morven. This was my first trip back home since Grandma had died and I had officially left the employment of Uncle Sam. NNU and I both made sure that I was the one driving the car as we entered Morven. Hey, look at me now! Not really.

I avoided as much as possible conversation about my early exit from the service. Most folks had some idea about what had gone down anyhow. A couple of my homeboys had also been stationed at Ft. Campbell during part of my stay there. There were comparisons drawn between me and Paul, who had also left the service early. During our two-day stay in North Carolina, NNU and I hung out mostly with Paul and his family. We did little visiting of my relatives that I recall. Part of it involved me being embarrassed about my service time being cut short, but I was also tripping slightly because of having brought this white woman home with me. Of course the talk about this white woman and me quickly circulated in the small community. Soon, we were having folks just happen by Paul's house to get a peek see. NNU was well received, for the most part, by the folks.

    I continued to get more and more carried away with my drunken escapades. As long as I half-way did what normal human beings do, NNU was willing to engage next door family who were not thrilled with her living with a black man. She also served notice to the local members of the Klan that she was not about to allow them to dictate her associations to her. In fact, we would wake one morning to a burning cross in the front yard. I was awed and pissed at the same time. Among the things running through my mind was: "This is the 1980s and folks are still burning crosses." I was truly disappointed with mankind. NNU would grab her 12 gauge shotgun and blow the base of the cross to smithereens, knocking it to the ground. I would stand there in that front yard for a while just watching the passing traffic that slowed, watching the neighbors that peered out from behind window curtains. There was no fear in me at that Moment. The question popped into my head though, "What the hell am I doing here?" There was no answer.

    NNU would eventually end up kicking me out of her place because of the frustrations created by my drinking and her having to deal with the ever present scrutiny of family and others. The final straw came with my wrecking her car while intoxicated one evening. I ended up in a one room efficiency apartment – across from the same VA Hospital. While NNU, at this point, had every right to be put out with me, she also enjoyed the position of presumed superiority over me. This became very clear to me. I also realized that I served as an opportunity for her to make amends in some sense for past sins. Her attempt to save me appeared to have failed.

A Geographical Cure

* * *

It was when I applied for a position in the VA Hospital's kitchen that I became aware that a schizophrenic diagnosis had, at some point, been attached to me. From all indications, the label was attached following my application for the job. The rationale for me not being offered the job was "hanging around other mentally disturbed people would cause you (because of your schizophrenic nature) to acclimate to their unhealthy behaviors." When I heard that, I knew someone had a personal problem with me. I also knew immediately that my rejection had to do with the relationship with NNU.

A little research revealed that a (white) psychiatrist who wrote the schizophrenic diagnosis label in my hospital chart, was a gentleman widely known within the hospital to have severe negative feelings about racially mixed dating, marriages, etc. Apparently his daughter had married a black man, against his objections. I do not recall ever having a session or conversation with this doctor.

I was hurt that power and position wrongly used could willfully be used to dictate the course of someone's life so easily. I would have been able to accept that job rejection a hell of a lot better if they had told me that I was not going to be hired because of alcohol being found in my system from the blood test that was done. I am sure that some was in my system at the time.

An attorney, BC, that had assisted me with my many legal dilemmas while in Murfreesboro, made a gallant effort to obtain those records from the hospital. The effort turned out to be to no avail. The purposely red-taped protocol eventually wore us down and we let the issue drop. The Walter Mitty in me wanted so badly to rise up – to smite down those responsible for this injustice. I appreciated BC's attempt to rectify legally, things for me. He was genuinely concerned about me. He was aware of my relationship with the white woman and he had in-depth knowledge of my drug using and other personal problems.

A steady job eventually came with the city's sewer department.

I worked third shift – until I was eventually fired from there – 'same ole thang' – nearly a year and a half later. I met EH, a black guy, at the plant who had been hired shortly before me. Almost immediately, EH and I began to hang out together after work. We both drank and smoked weed, but he was also into shooting up with what we called T's and Blues. EH had spent time in the service as well. I was impressed with his machoism, his ability to pick up girls, the social ease he had with nearly everyone he met, and his ability to function when high. EH and I would travel the night club circuits in Murfreesboro and Nashville. Unless I was totally inebriated, the same anxieties that wore me out trying to hang out with the boys of old were prevalent. Though he was a nice guy for the most part, he did have a problem getting over on people, however. If he perceived himself as having been disrespected, EH would react with whatever mode of comeback necessary (verbal or physical aggression) to make his point.

 A huge piece of me admired EH's ability to pull the girls whenever we were out together. I envied his ability to do so. It was a skill that I had never been able to grasp while sober. I would watch him work the young ladies, eventually making the sexual connection with the one of his choosing. In the meantime, I would want to do the same, but would end up being frustrated with my lack of nerve and drink myself into oblivion. EH would often share his sexual conquest with me, those that had occurred when we were not hanging out together. He would even occasionally offer me the opportunity to score with those that had been a one shot deal with him. What pride I did have at that time kept me from following up on all but one of those opportunities. That particular young lady would end up getting sick, throwing up, from having shot up with T's and Blues, putting a major damper on the occasion. I'd struck out again, in a sense. I would leave that situation feeling like if I didn't have bad luck, I would have no luck at all.

 EH would explain his less than choir boy demeanor to having had to grow up with relatives because his birth mother had thrown him in a dumpster when he was a baby. "I'm gonna get all I can from whoever I can while I can," he would say occasionally when high and it was just the two of us. I could hear the hurt and anger in his voice when that statement rolled out of him. I knew that EH used me on occasions for drugs, money, transportation, etc. He was someone who half-way tolerated me and my drunken stupors and irrational behaviors. I was aware that he viewed me as being weak, and in reality, I was. But not until we were about to go our separate ways (he, heading over to Germany where he had been stationed most of his army tour) did he stop making the effort not to show it. I would allow him to embarrass me on numerous occasions in the presence of mutual acquaintances – without retribution (sounds familiar). We both shared similar hurts and pains. EH did a much better job of controlling and directing his. To a large degree, he was in control; in my case, despite my sober exterior cool demeanor, I had little control of mine.

Over a three-year period, I would manage to wind up in jail for such charges as public drunk; DUI; possession; and assault, a total of more than ten times. My driver's license would be suspended for a year as well. After wrecking a third vehicle, I acquired a 26-inch bicycle, with a 2.5 horsepower Sears motor on the front wheel as my primary mode of transportation. The fear of me driving drunk and killing someone became very real to me during that time. The bike was actually suggested by NNU. Forget being macho and doing what a man should do. I had been thoroughly beaten down, not enough to stop drinking and actively seek to treat the pain and misery within me, but worn down nevertheless. I rode/ drove the bike to the grocery store, to the bank, to the nightclub, to the job, to the liquor store. I eventually ended up selling the bike for $90.00 worth of (bootleg) liquor to a cab driver, who I would end up in jail with one night following our heavy drinking and cathouse adventuring.

Shingle roofing, washing dishes in the little restaurant in the front of the building where I lived, working construction with the building's owner, and bill- board placement were among the other jobs I would go through during that period of time. All of those jobs were offered by people in an attempt to help me out. The shingle roofing turned out to be an adventure as I moved from carrying shingles to the roof for the other guys to actually putting them on.

That was a novelty. Apparently, at that time no other black person in Rutherford County had done such a thing. I resented having had to talk Bobby L., into getting me into actual roofing in the first place. I resented even more the prevailing thought in that area that black folks were not smart enough to accurately nail shingles on a roof. White folks would make it a point to drive by the site we would be working on, just to see the nigger laying down shingles alongside the white boys. What was the world coming to?

I vividly remember the back breaking work of manually digging six-feet holes to put up highway and interstate billboard signs. Being paid only six dollars an hour didn't provide much motivation either. Even with gloves on, my hand wore blisters at the end of the day. The guy I was working for, Tony L, was a white fellow who indirectly held his obvious superiority intellect out for me to view. For the money he was being paid to erect those signs, he could have bestowed a little more my way. He viewed himself as helping out this down and out black fellow. He was pretty sure that I would accept whatever he offered to pay me. He was right. Do not misunderstand me, I am appreciative for the Tony Ls and the Bobby Ls giving me the opportunity to survive financially during those times, but I can't help but be bothered by the one human being better than another human being undercurrents as well.

* * *

My first attempt to stop drinking after joining Alcoholics Anonymous (AA) lasted about three months. The sobriety was not real because I still chose to continue smoking marijuana during that three-month period. The lesson was learned that I could not do a secondary mood-altering drug without eventually returning to that primary drug. And of course, the return visits to jail resumed in short order. In the meantime, I was being kicked out of my efficiency apartment, while applying to and being accepted into the Graduate School Psychology Program at Middle Tennessee State University (MTSU). I was to find out later that NNU had taken it upon herself to talk to the judge who presided over my assault charge. According to her, she had told him about my potential and my acceptance into MTSU and had convinced him not to impose the standard 10- month/ 29-day jail time that appeared to be in order since that was my second time before him. However, NNU would make this revelation to me in an attempt to keep me in our on again-off again unhealthy relationship. She would tell me about her visit to the judge during my last semester at MTSU.

I was kicked out of my apartment supposedly because of my being a nuisance to the other tenants in the surrounding complex – when drunk, which was a frequent occurrence. When I was not drinking, I would simply speak to the white folks and go on and on. However, when king alcohol had its grip on me, I wanted to socialize a bit more than what the white women and their husbands or boyfriends were comfortable with. For the most part, folks knew that I was harmless, but then again I was a black man in the presence of white women. The local redneck would confront me at the telephone booth near the highway one evening after a complaint of being frightened by me, came from one of those white women. The one white boy would back his car up brushing my thigh, jump out of his car brandishing a hunting knife. He placed the knife under my throat as he delivered his message about me staying away from those white women. As he held the knife to my throat I glanced over at his partner sitting in his pickup truck with his door opened so that I could see the .22 caliber rifle he had bouncing ever so gently up and down in his hands. The guy in the pickup nodded his head slowly back and forth, eyeing me and nonverbally saying to me, not to attempt any resistance with his friend. So I heeded his unspoken advice and let this fool slam blast me; I let him humiliate me.

During this brief period of time, a ton of people, white and black, rode by in their vehicles. Out of the corner of my eye, I could notice the white folks slowing down to a near crawl to fully take in the scene, while the black folks tended to maintain and even increase their speed as they came by and realized what was happening. After approximately 7 to 8 minutes (which seemed more like 7 or 8 hours), the white boys, satisfied that they straightened this nigger out, hauled-ass back toward Lebanon. I had just started a conversation with an acquaintance when the ordeal began. All this time I still held the phone in my right hand; it never occurred to me to hang it up. More accurately, I was not about to take my eyes or my focus off the white boys during that time. Obviously, my acquaintance overheard the entire deal. I was even more embarrassed. I recall feeling more anger than fear. I wanted to whip that white boy's behind so badly I could taste it. I would walk up to the little store on the next corner about a half mile up the road and wait for my acquaintance to come pick me up.

* * *

I would end up moving in with NNU while waiting to move onto the MTSU campus. My friend only agreed to this because I promised her that I would not drink during my brief stay. I lied. I had the wife of my cab driver buddy (he had been kicked out of house and home by then) meet me at the local library one morning with two half pints of whiskey (they normally didn't stock vodka). NNU had dropped me off there, supposedly to check out a book to read, constructively passing the time until school started. After running a few errands, my friend returned to the library to pick me up and take me back to her place. I hid the two bottles of whiskey in my socks. As soon as she left for work that afternoon, I got busy with the whiskey. I did absolutely no reading of the book that I had checked out. By the time NNU got home from work that evening around 11:30 p.m., I was feeling no pain. Like radar, she came directly to the couch where I was lying after entering the trailer door. She leaned over me, putting her nose to my face, just like back in the hospital that one afternoon. The alcohol smell was, indeed, upon me. Of course NNU was angry and threatened to kick me out. After ranting for a few minutes, she calmed down and backed off from the threat. There was only a week to go before registration.

* * *

A Geographical Cure

In January 1984, I began my graduate studies at Middle Tennessee State University. I was drunk when I went to register for classes that day, but I was able to function well enough to get the job done. I had secured a pint of whiskey earlier in the day, again from my cab buddy. I had hidden it in one of my old army field jacket pockets. I moved into my dorm room, sharing it was a mild-mannered white dude named Keith. He had no idea what he was in for. It did not take Keith long to realize that he had a drunk and a fool for a roommate, who only stayed sober long enough to attend classes, and that was a temporary state of existence. Immediately after my last class of the day, I would head to the liquor store located directly across from the North end of campus, with my black book bag. I would return to my room with the goods and drink myself silly. After reaching that point, I would be off to the local tavern, also situated within walking distance of the school. There, in my drunken stupors, I would irritate folks, particularly the young ladies, unmercifully. Again, I could not make the approach for their company without being intoxicated.

Many an evening study and homework went undone. My roommate, fed up with my drunken antics, would eventually turn me in to campus housing authorities. In fact, he worked at the university housing office! This would happen several times by the time that first semester was over. I would get busted by campus security for having alcohol in my possession, which was a no-no. Actually, the institution was tolerant of such, as long as we were not blatant about "partying". I would walk around the dorm court area openly drinking beer (of course I would be drunk, otherwise, I had a little more sense about me). Another time I would embarrass the school by having the Murfreesboro police arrest me on campus for having been a passenger in a hit and run accident.

The guy driving the car, a local brother whom I had recently met, struck another vehicle traveling on Memorial Boulevard (down town) late one evening, panicked, and sped off. He headed straight back toward the MTSU campus. I could hear a siren fall in behind us after we had gone about half a mile. We were both high and scared as hell. By the time we came to a stop in my dorm parking lot, we were surrounded by the fuzz. The cops graciously did not charge me with possession that time, though they found a small amount of marijuana on me when they caught up with us back on campus. I was eventually released later that evening since I was not driving the car. Being a graduate student helped me considerably. On my way to class the next morning, I knew by the looks that the word about last night had gotten around.

Billy Joel's *I Am An Innocent Man* was out the Winter of 1984. Every time that song came across the airways, my emotional pain level increased two-fold.

The words of the song intensified the longing in me to be loved, to be understood, to be accepted. Whenever I visited the local black hangouts, the folks usually would watch me get drunk, and then watch me react to the music on the jukebox. My reputation was thoroughly entrenched in the Murfreesboro community by then. I could maintain fairly well with most of the "heart-thumping" sounds when the alcohol had put me into the land of the un-cool. J. Blackfoot's song,

Taxi, did me in every time though. I could occasionally hear the folks saying "watch him now" when that number came on. The longing and the pain inside me seemed to magnify to baseball size.

I would occasionally get ripped off of money, dope, etc., during those times. The vultures would lay in wait for me to get drunk. I would sometimes wake up in strange, unfamiliar parts of the city, broke of course, not knowing how I had gotten there. I was at the club or an apartment, was my last recollection. There is no doubt now that the Spirit was surely protecting me from (serious) physical harm during those adventures. *God takes care of babies and fools.*

* * *

By the time October 1984 rolled around the MTSU, in no mincing of words, was asking me to leave their institution. Either go get help for my problem and return to complete my studies or be gone altogether! The final straw had occurred when I accidentally set my dorm room on fire – while drunk, of course.

I had worked an eight hour shift at the University Grill that evening, Saturday, October 5, 1984, and was overjoyed when we finally closed up shop. DT, one of my co-workers, and I went straight to the liquor store, purchased a bag of weed from a guy off campus and proceeded back to my room on campus. Both DT and I had gone through a fifth of vodka each and had smoked several joints when I decided to put hot dogs on the stove to help pacify our growing hunger. Neither of us was paying much attention. Suddenly there would be a blaze, and a pillar of smoke would rise up from the range. A short time later a smoke alarm would go off. DT would jump up at that point and grab his remaining bottle of liquor and the remaining marijuana and hurriedly exit the room.

The next thing I recall is the fire department, paramedics, and the police showing up at the dorm. The fire was quickly extinguished. Someone spotted my two-thirds/half-full (second fifth) of vodka on the floor next to the coffee table. The two empty bottles (one belonging to DT) would be observed next to my stereo system. At that point the questions would begin. The paramedics decided that I stood a chance of stroking out from all the apparent drinking and would rush me to the local hospital. There they would conduct a blood-alcohol test that revealed a level of 3.5. A doctor would give me a shot in my left arm of an unknown (to me) substance to offset the possibility of a heart attack. It would not occur to me until sober later, that with nearly another fifth left and me having every intention of finishing it, with my BAC already dangerously high, that probably had inadvertently saved my life that evening. The Spirit at work again.

I would be taken back to campus after achieving some measure of stabilization early Sunday morning. I would spend the entire day in my room in a semi-haze, experiencing ETOH withdrawal symptoms. I never saw or heard from DT again. Someone told me after my treatment that he had dropped out of school and moved to Texas. MTSU administration came calling for me mid-Monday morning. They would make their ultimatum and give me the remainder of the day to make arrangements to get help. I did not attend classes that day and may have stuck my head out the door for a very brief period, once or twice at most. I was sure word had long since gotten around campus about my latest escapade. My roommate at that time, along with his girlfriend, showed both compassion and pity. They made it a point to simply stay out of my way. Seeing my pain and embarrassment, he made it a point to keep the curious away from the apartment also. I was grateful.

* * *

Earlier during the summer school session, the institution had encouraged me to enter the Union Mission Recovery Program in Nashville. Such a recommendation had come about after the fourth or fifth time I had been caught with alcohol on campus and a couple of other things on top of those. My roommate that summer had done a lot of complaining about me as well. A friend of this particular roommate, a druggie himself, thought that I was the biggest trip he had ever met. Just for the hell of it, these folks would put firecrackers on the floor next to the head of my bed one night after I had come in drunk and had passed out. I would finally awake as the last of the packet of firecrackers were going off. Realizing what had happened, I got up from my bed and quickly ran to the apartment front door – just in time to get a glimpse of my roommate's friend turning the corner of the courtyard, laughing his head off in the process. That same roommate used to periodically pour my booze out whenever I became fully incapacitated. It did not take him long not to be impressed with me. I simply freaked the young white boy out.

The administration had also received not so sterling reports about me from the psychology department, mostly concerning me showing up for classes intoxicated. My professors certainly were not pleased. Here I was in their graduate program displaying the type of disturbing and unsettling behavior they were training me to serve. It was not going to fly with them. I don't remember who took me to Nashville on that particular occasion (I was drunk and in a blackout), but after arriving there late one afternoon, I would walk through the Mission with bag in hand and back on the street. I had returned to a state of consciousness long enough to realize where I was. I would hang out on the street, skid row, get drunk some more, and, eventually pass out on the sidewalk in front of the Mission.

I would wake up about 4:00 a.m. the following morning and go with one of the other guys on the street to a nearby house and purchase a bottle of Thunderbird.

It didn't take much at that point to get drunk all over again. By the time dawn arrived and the city was beginning to stir with the normal folks going off to work, a couple of my new found friends and I were off to sell blood – to get money for breakfast and beer. It seemed to be such a natural thing to do.

I recall a homeless fellow telling me while we sipped a beer after breakfast, that what I had experienced since my arrival the day before was basically how he and others spent their time on the street, one day after another, over and over again, until something happened to one of them. Very few of them ever made it out. Around mid-afternoon, my money and alcohol were gone again. I decided at that point that it was time for my return to MTSU. What further convinced me to return to Murfreesboro was a scene that I had been guided into by one of those fellows where we were going to hang out for a while at some little makeshift apartment. The guy had said that there was a couple that lived there, that generally kept booze in stock. We walked through the front door and there on the couch is the couple, two guys who are totally nude, hugging and caressing one another.

The air in the room was thick with a funky sexual body odor already on that hot summer morning. My stomach turned upside down and then back up again. I could not believe what I saw, nor inhaled. My homophobia quickly kicked in, as feelings of fear and disgust jointly came over me. It was time for me to go.

I talked a taxi driver into taking me to Murfreesboro – on credit (until I could get back to my dorm room and retrieve and pawn my portable tape player). Naturally, my roommate and other folks on campus were surprised to see me back so soon. In fact, my roommate would end up moving out of the apartment the same evening. Because of the Associate Dean of Students, John David Hays, the institution allowed me to stay. He had, time and time again, given me breaks when I found myself before him for my drunken campus exploits. John David had protected me from the University hounds who had long since wanted me gone. I was given another opportunity to make good on my primary purpose for being there. I was good to go…until that final screw-up later that October.

* * *

My father had died earlier that same summer. Paul would call me from North Carolina to tell me. Both of us were silent for a few seconds after he initially relayed the news. I knew that the days of old – of the abuse were flashing back in his mind, as they were mine. I felt much of the same anger I always felt toward my father, even though I had not seen him in at least 15 years. My mind would flash back to that final time I had seen him all those years earlier. I had to have been 13 or 14 years old. Vick had blindsided me one afternoon on the corner. I had no idea he was in Morven, let alone on the block. I heard his voice first. The standard hey boy…rattled into my eardrums. This is not real I thought as I turned in the direction of the Darth Vader tone. Sure enough, my father was within four yards of me and was approaching, slowly and cautiously. An immediate surge of anger rose within me when I made eye contact with him. I charged him – with the intent of inflicting some serious bodily harm on him. The fact that I was out- aged, out-weighed, and out-sized never entered my mind. One of the boys quickly stepped in between me and my father, moving me a few feet in the opposite direction. The man with Vick pulled him back to a waiting car, mumbling something to the effect of "leave the boy alone". My father had a stunned look on his face and made no attempt to say anything else. Unable to say a word either, I eyed him as he climbed back into the car and headed toward Wadesboro. I never saw him again.

I felt absolutely no sadness because he had died. There was no joy either, but certainly at that time there were no regrets. I refused to attend his funeral. Paul did not attend either. My co-workers and supervisors at the Kroger store I worked at that summer were set to donate the funds to get me to New Jersey, the funeral site, and back. I would refuse to accept their generosity. Of course many of them did not understand my refusal, nor could they understand my lack of visible grief. I did not bother to explain. Perhaps I owed them an explanation, but the motivation to deliver one was not in me. I knew I had some serious work to do in terms of letting go and forgiving Vick Wall, but I was nowhere near being ready to begin such a trek at that time. I knew it would be a difficulty journey, as it has, indeed, proven to be.

I got seriously drunk that evening after I got off from work. I ended up passing out in my dorm room, waking up the next morning sprawled out on the floor. A puddle of the remaining liquor that I had not finished in the half gallon jug was deposited on the floor next to me. I intentionally stayed away from folks that day, until I could not avoid it because of having to go back to work. Actually, my supervisor and the store's manager had offered me time off to deal with whatever needed to be dealt with. I had refused that also.

* * *

John David Hays took a personal day off from work that Tuesday to drive me down to the Samaritan Treatment Center – for a 30 day drug cessation program.

He knew that if someone did not personally take me to Nashville, I would opt to hit the streets of Murfreesboro and ... The institution would allow me to put my graduate coursework on hold while I completed treatment. I would lose none of the credits I had already earned.

Monday, October 7, 1984, was the last time I took a drink of alcohol or used other mind/mood-altering drugs for the purpose of getting high. Approximately two shots of vodka were in a glass in the refrigerator; I turned up the glass and emptied its contents with one bend of the elbow. I have no idea what happened to the remainder of that second fifth. All I knew was my nerves were shot; I was an emotional and mental wreck as I entered the Center. And, yes, I wanted to die….but not really…just to stop hurting. I would be paying for my stay there by way of monies from a student loan. The Samaritan Center was not considered to be among the elite in terms of the modern-day treatment facility and its physical amenities, but it had a well-deserved reputation of helping folks to develop long- term sobriety. It would certainly prove to be the place the Spirit wanted me to be.

6
The Miracle

There comes a time
when I must choose to be Responsible for Me;
in spite of who did what to me;
whether I had the things I was supposed to have had or not.
I cannot Blame; I cannot Hate; I cannot Choose to Fail
Because others Failed me.

There comes a time
when I must choose to be Responsible for Me;
choosing to use God's Precious Gifts;
choosing to be a positive force in this world;
choosing to Love myself and others;
choosing to Believe in me;
choosing to fulfill my destiny.

There comes a time when I must choose to be Responsible for Me - That time is now.

—CDW

My nerves had only begun to calm down minimally by Friday of the first week of my stay at The Samaritan Center. Especially during the meals of mostly soup and sandwiches my hands would shake uncontrollably. This was partly due to me detoxing from the alcohol and partly because of an internal panic button that would still activate when the eyes of others were on me. I generally had very little to say during the several groups and meetings that we had each day. I listened as best I could between feeling bad physically, emotionally, mentally, and spiritually. Most of us clients involved in the 30-day program appeared out of touch during those early days.

There were a couple of guys and one young lady that I loosely attached myself to. We all seemed to be searching for the one thing that had eluded us over the course of our time – inner peace. The young lady, Sarah, was the more vocal of our little inner circle. She spoke a great deal about her negative experiences with family and world growing up in Pittsburgh. Her voice was always laced with standard pain and anger. Sarah still had the ability to smile occasionally and appeared to be an entirely different person when she did. David was more laid back. In sharing a little about himself, we quickly realized that the level of his inner turmoil was just as great as the rest of us. David was obviously an intelligent fellow, but as is typical with many lost souls at that stage of being, he did not know how to consistently access that inner brilliance. We all showed the tremendous need to want to care enough to fight for ourselves. Pure motivation to make that initial step on the journey to true self was coming with a great deal of difficulty.

A couple of the Center counseling staff and one of its nurses had some serious attitudes toward me. I would become convinced later, mostly by inadvertent comments made, that this was true primarily because of my enrollment in graduate school. I guess that would boil down to jealousy. Very few of them had a Masters Degree. Why that bothered them as much as it apparently did still dumbfounded me. It was more disappointing than anything else. How can you assist others in discovering themselves if you cannot see past yourself? But that was okay, because I had made up my mind during the ride to the Center on Tuesday morning that I would allow them to do whatever they wanted to do to me or with me, mentally and emotionally. I had laid myself bare for this treatment venture.

We were exercising in group, attending AA meetings, and consuming soup and sandwiches, along with antibuse, an alcohol-use deterrent. The nurse would seize an opportunity to slam blast me one afternoon while we were receiving our daily dose of medication. I had proceeded to pick up my pill from the med tray without her official consent. She would scold me as if I were a child. "Who do you think your are?" she would yell in the presence of everyone. I mumbled an apology out between my waves of humiliation. There was no fight back or resistance, even though I knew her reaction was more personal than professional. I give her credit though for catching herself halfway through the tirade and shutting down. I remember standing there looking at her with near tears in my eyes while she spoke. I think that it was her recognizing the pain and embarrassment that I stood there with that pushed her to discontinue her verbal onslaught.

By Friday afternoon, the hurt, pain, and depression seemed to magnify immensely. My mind raced back and forth between thoughts of suicide, running away from the Center, and getting drunk. I remember standing on the hill that overlooked 4th Avenue visualizing making the move to temporarily (or permanently) ease the pain. But only by the Grace of God did I not leave there or do something else stupid that Friday evening. I hung out with Sarah, David and a dude from Murfreesboro pretty much that entire weekend. It was not so much me making the effort to hang out with them. It was more like we all intuitively knew that we needed to hang out together that weekend. We all survived it.

The second week held pretty much the same in terms of the treatment regimen.

My head had cleared somewhat and the overt shakes had gradually left me. Friday came around again. I recall consciously making this statement to myself in my head: "I will not allow myself to hurt this weekend like I did last weekend." The remainder of that weekend, Friday evening through Monday morning, is a blur to me. I truly have no recollection of specifics over those three days.

I remember walking out of the residence hall on Monday morning and someone asked how I was doing. I stopped with the question and responded simply, "serene". To my knowledge, that word had never come out of my mouth prior to that Moment. Whoever had asked me the question went on into the building for breakfast. I stood there, not caring at all about how odd I must have looked ? just standing there in the middle of the courtyard. There was a warm feeling in my chest (not heartburn either) that I had never felt before. I tried not to think about it much, out of fear of losing such an awesome feeling. For the rest of that day and over the next several days, in fact every time anyone would ask how I was doing, I responded with "serene. "For the first time in my life, I felt a measure of real peace within me; for the first time, I felt a small measure of self-love. And I knew that IT was a gift from God. It felt so good that I instinctively made a promise to myself right then and there that I would do whatever I had to do to maintain and met more of IT. I would also do whatever I could to help others who might be struggling to come to a similar point in their lives. A miracle? Yes, it was, indeed, a miracle ? of gigantic proportions. And I was on my way to discovering my true self. As author, Andy Cohen notes: *"....the Moment we get an idea of peace, confusion leaves us....and just as a little leaven leavens the whole loaf, so will even a little* change in our manner of thinking, from the negative to the affirmative, affect *the whole course and nature of our everyday life."*

* * *

With that very special experience, all my problems didn't suddenly disappear; but I knew that in time I would get better. I realized that I could not have possibly done serious, effective work on my pain while I was still using mood altering chemicals. My healing was just beginning. In AA meetings and in group sessions I noticed that I began to speak more often on a voluntary basis. I began to speak with more depth, with more hope, with more confidence. I had begun to be real.

I had begun what would be a lifelong march toward loving and accepting me unconditionally, which was to include a great deal of forgiving myself. It would be nearly a year later before I would, for the first time in my life, feel and then announce I finally felt a part of the human race, and I deserved to be here – as much as anyone else.

But I also wanted everything right then! I want what I want when I want it, right now! That had always been an underlying modus operandi for me. And my desire to grow and to heal overnight, I knew, had to be tempered with reality and the recognition and acceptance that such things would happen on God's timetable, not mine. After those years of searching for love, in everything and everybody else, it was more than a pleasant revelation to come to the understanding, as in the words of a popular George Benson song: *The greatest love of all is inside of* me.

* * *

After completing the initial 30-day program, I had decided to move into the transitional phase of treatment. I had decided to just stay at the Center until January, when I was scheduled to re-enter MTSU. I had set up shop in the transitional living quarters and was becoming more and more comfortable with myself and those around me. About a month into that second treatment phase, I would be asked to leave the Center. Here we go again. That command did not diminish my gratitude for the earlier miracle that had been granted me.

I was asked to leave because of a false accusation by a couple of the female clients that supposedly revolved around me threatening and intimidating them. One of those girls turned out to be my buddy, Sarah. I would not be allowed to confront her before leaving. In what way, I was never quite sure. The charge was not true. I remembered Sarah having gotten upset with me earlier that day at breakfast, presumably because of the noticeable difference in my response to her greeting versus another young lady who joined us at the same table. My response to Sarah's good morning was low key and tinted with disappointment – because of her having gone out with a local guy who I perceived as not being good for her. Perhaps I was jealous of the guy rather than concerned about her well being.

I was not sure which was more accurate. After my more gleeful greeting to the other young lady, Sarah would become enraged and loudly state something to the effect, "I'm tired of this shit!" She would get up and move to another table. Though I was slightly embarrassed and even more surprised, I played it off and completed my breakfast in near silence. I would not see Sarah again after that breakfast.

It would be around mid-morning when I would be called into the Center Director's office and presented with the accusation. I was stunned. Most of the folks who became aware of it knew that it was not true. One guy would try to tell me that a lot if it had to do with the way I carried myself, particularly when upset. Apparently, I walked with a much more profound swagger, more erect, more stoic. It was obvious that I was angry about something or with someone. Sarah and the same lady who had sat with me at breakfast earlier were conspicuously absent from lunch. Obviously, they were the two that had leveled the charge against me. I remember having very little interaction period with this other girl.

I knew that a couple members of the staff would seize the opportunity to push for my ouster, and they were successful. By mid-afternoon I was being asked to leave the institution. After attempting to explain my side of the story, and it being rejected, though hurt and disappointed I resigned myself to the fact it was time to go. The Spirit reassured me that it was time to go, and I knew I was going to be okay. Even though it was stated by one of the Center staff that I was headed for a drunk (the explanation given to a group after my departure), I knew that such was not going to happen as long as I did my part in maintaining that new found connection with God and myself.

Lest I leave anyone with the impression that The Samaritan Center staff was all out to get me, that was certainly not the case. I believe that everybody there were doing and being as they were supposed to be doing and being. Nothing in my world happens by accident. I have much gratitude to counselors John P., and Carla for always forcing me to be honest with myself, in spite of my desire to manipulate and subtly control, and to Mrs. Audrey D., in administration, for gracefully communicating a never wavering acceptance of me from the outset of my journey there. I will be eternally grateful to Dr. Samantha M., for not accepting the unreal, the show part of me and for her pushing me to a point of realness. Thoroughly etched in my mind is the group session in which she asked me the question; "Curtis, how do you know when something is right for you to do?" I thought for a brief Moment and responded: "When it feels right." Dr. Samantha M., stared a look of approval at me, smiled slightly, and then said, "You're going to be okay." It was then that I knew she had been ripping me apart because she liked me and wanted me to get better. Our once self-perceived strained relationship was forever changed at that Moment.

Dr. Samantha M., was away from the Center at the time of my being asked to leave. Curiously, one of her final statements to me the day she left on vacation was, "You make sure you're here when I return." This lady was, indeed, keen and insightful. Did she have an inkling of something like this awaiting me? The thought of me fighting to hang around for her return crossed my mind. Not that my doing more than what I did in defending myself would have made any difference. Seeing her again before my leaving would have been worth the effort. But again, I knew that it was my time to leave.

It was approximately a week before I was to re-enter school. After packing and saying a few goodbyes, I got a cab to take me back to Murfreesboro. He dropped me off at one of the local motels. I would stay there until school started.

I spent a lot of time by myself, attended AA meetings on a daily basis. I had called NNU to let her know that I was back in town. She stopped by to visit me a couple of times during the week. I could tell by her reactions to me to similar past situations that she knew something had changed about me. I was okay.

I was going to be okay. I had some sense of who I was. Therefore, I was nowhere near as needy emotionally as I had been before.

7
Letting Go and Moving On

"At a certain point in life we must be willing to live in a new world – one which affirms that we are not deserving of punishment, but of self-respect, freedom, and celebration."

— Author Unknown

I would return to MTSU a different person. It only took a short while for my fellow graduate students, professors, and dorm mates to realize the change. The folks I used to occasionally party with were amazed at the transformation. After the initial period of testing me (asking me to get high) and my constant refusal to do so, they would eventually stop asking. They began to feel comfortable with my new way of being. The word living is by no means a small one, because up until the miracle at The Samaritan Center, I had only existed in this world.

And make no mistake about it, there is a tremendous difference between the two. Mere existence involves going through each day with no true enjoyment of life and no hope that the next day is going to be any better than today. Living, however, signifies that one is getting the most out of each day, growing from life's ups and downs, and there exists a deep, emblazoned belief that "life is, in fact, a journey rather than a destination."

* * *

During my stay at The Samaritan Center, the staff and clients had given me a 30th birthday party. That was significant because it was the first time in my life my birthday had ever been acknowledged and formally celebrated. The occasion marked one of the best feelings I had ever had. I got the feeling that there were several other clients there who understood the significance of the Moment for me. Though there were no tears, my insides were swollen to capacity – with joy, gratitude and disbelief. There was the usual cake and ice cream, in addition to a few simple gifts. I do not even recall what the gifts were because the real gift had been those folks simply taking the time to acknowledge me on that occasion.

My eventual acceptance back into the university community brought about a similar feeling. "Wow, these folks like me!" I will always have a deep appreciation for their willingness to give me another chance. Many thanks to John David, and to Jane Tipps, one of the school's guidance counselors, for staying with me through that period of trying transformation ? before, during, and after my treatment venture. It became apparent during those times that God had always put people in my life at Moments when I most needed someone, no matter how miserable my life seemed to be at that particular time. My survival up to that point had been no accident. Though I was yet to have a clear vision of my purpose in life, I began to slowly understand that all the pain and negative experiences were groundwork for that purpose.

* * *

I would meet the lady I would end up marrying during my second year back at MTSU. I had always longed to meet that special somebody. I had a mental list of what I wanted this special one to be like, and Evelyn would meet all requirements. The first time I saw her she walked toward me as I sat outside waiting between classes. We spoke and acknowledged each other at about the same time. I would ask her before I knew it, "Are you a teacher here?" That was definitely how she carried herself. We did not officially introduce ourselves to one another at that time. She was certainly a true vision of loveliness. My heart was off and running at that Moment. We saw each other a few times in passing over the next couple of weeks. I would come to find out later that Evelyn had seen me coming on several occasions and had gone the other way to avoid me.

She had been under the impression that I was just another younger, under-classman taken with her.

I would officially introduce myself to her one afternoon – before she was able to retreat in another direction. I walked up to her and said something like, "I want to officially introduce myself; my name is Curtis D. Wall and I am a tremendously fascinating human being." She would look (smiling a bit) as if I was slightly off and say her name. We chit-chatted about our majors and then proceeded on our separate ways. I did not have the nerve or confidence to ask her for a phone number. One Saturday morning about a week and a half later, while in the student center checking my mailbox, I would run into Evelyn and her daughter, Chloe, from a previous marriage. Something in me said that I had better seize the opportunity. After exchanging pleasantries I would ask her for her phone number. She would look me straight in the eye and respond, "No, you're too young and I'm not interested." Rather than my heart sinking from another rejection, I quickly thought to pull my driver's license from my wallet, flashing my date of birth (Good thing I had one!). She would then relate that she had no idea I was that old. Without thinking, I would calmly state, "Yes, I am; now, give me your phone number, please." She did and I called her about a week later ... and the rest is history.

Even though I wanted to get emotionally close to Evelyn, the fear and uncertainty in doing so was present also. In fact, when I became aware of where we both appeared to be headed, I would sit her down and detail much of the information included in this book about my past. She would listen without comment for the most part. After that evening, I would not hear from her for about a week. Evelyn would later tell me that I had almost lost her then for she had been raised in a stable Christian home, and a lot of what I told her about myself was truly frightening to her. I am not sure, even now, if I did not tell her those things in an attempt to scare her away because I was afraid of going to such an emotional level. Only she came back!

We would become engaged prior to our leaving MTSU in 1986. That would be another monstrous move for me. After all, I was the Lone Wolf, one who was really afraid of a committed relationship, though I had been constantly searching for one. As the engagement story goes, we were talking on the phone one afternoon, several days prior to our heading in different directions. I remember telling her that I wanted to give her a gift that represented us being more than just friends. Evelyn would come back with, "But Curtis, you have not asked me to marry you!" Though marriage was not quite what I had in mind, I came back immediately with, "So, will you?" She responded with a yes and I was off to the pawn shop to hock a gold necklace in order to purchase an official engagement ring. The pawn shop had the ring that I was intending to give her. I knew that when I saw it; and there was just enough money to make the buy.

The Spirit led me to Arlington Developmental Center, as a Psychological Examiner. The Center was situated in the small town of Arlington, TN, approximately 20 miles from downtown Memphis. I had originally planned to attend the University of Tennessee at Knoxville, to work on my Ph.D., but the Spirit had other plans for me. There was no doubt in my being that I was supposed to come to the Memphis, TN area at that time. Evelyn and Chloe would head to Chattanooga, to begin work for an insurance agency. Over the next six months, we would see each other two or three times on weekend visits. Of course, we talked to each other frequently by phone. Evelyn's job would fizzle out in Chattanooga around early December. Her father and I would convince her to move up our scheduled wedding date from September of that following year to January 1987. She needed convincing since she did not want to come to the union without a job, but her father and I won out. It was to be.

I went through most of that time immediately prior to the wedding in a daze. But I truly believed that she was the person God wanted me to marry. I still believe that, in spite of some difficult times along this trek. We would marry on January 1, 1987, choosing to ignore the tax benefits of doing it earlier. She and Chloe would move to Memphis with me after a brief honeymoon. Chloe had difficulty in the beginning accepting me as her real father (particularly when she was angry with me), but she would ask to become legally a Wall as an 8th birthday present. That made me feel good. I do not like using the terminology of stepdaughter in referring to her. For surely in my heart, she is mine. My son, Curtis Jr., would be born on July 28, 1988. Evelyn and I did not get married and then live happily ever after, as you will sample later in this expose. There have been times of struggle from both having brought excess baggage into the union. Moving from love to real love has been a job. But because of the intra and interpersonal growth, the journey has been worth it.

* * *

I would also buy the second car of my lifetime at the beginning of the last semester at MTSU. I used student loan funds to purchase a 1972 Toyota Celica from an elderly white gentleman for $750.00. The bodywork was faded and it had a large dent on the driver's side where it had been wrecked. That was okay, I could live with that. The Celica was gold in color and another 5 speed, no less. This time though, I had no difficulty acclimating myself to the car. I would spend around $900.00 having the engine redone. I went any and everywhere I needed to go in that car. Neither rain nor sleet nor snow could stop me in that Toyota! And I did properly register the vehicle, getting insurance and all. What a difference a miracle makes. I would end up selling the car for $300.00 to a struggling couple new to the city of Memphis, where I had set up shop.

By attending both summer sessions in 1995, I had been able to graduate in May of 1996 along with my peers, the ones I had begun that journey with in January 1994. I had regained their respect, as well as the respect of my professors and the Psychology Department as a whole. Many of them were proud of me. I felt good. I was even able to allow a few of those folks to stand alongside that emotional keep-away wall of mine. Today, I treasure those times. Completing the necessary course work, finishing my thesis, and passing comps in order to be eligible to walk across that stage were not nearly the most important accomplishment during my return to MTSU.

I found the strength to step completely away from the unhealthy relationship with NNU and eventually enter another in spite of my fears. A tremendous sense of relief came over me when I stood firm that final time while NNU pressured me not to walk away. She would make an impassioned threat about getting a shotgun and blowing my brains out. I invited her to do just that. At that particular Moment I was being true to me, no matter what the consequences. Also, I'm sure that I knew that the threat was not one NNU would likely follow through with. I remember her assuring me that at some point in the future I would get drunk and come back to her. After those final words, we were a done deal. By the Grace of God, such a thing has not come to pass. Despite the unhealthiness of the relationship, I know that NNU was purposely placed in my world at a time – when I needed that particular someone to stave off any successful attempt on my part to exit this planet before my time. So I have no malice toward her and wish her the best that life has to offer.

At least once a month back then I would still go through periods of depression that lasted anywhere from three to ten days. Even that was an improvement over the near constant desolation that I'd felt prior to my miracle. Always in the back of my head, in spite of what my emotional state was, a little voice kept telling me that everything was going to be okay. At no time did I have a desire to get high, get drunk or take myself away from the depression via mood-altering chemicals. My emotional, mental, and spiritual states gradually came to be more healthy and more real within me, one day at a time.

* * *

Approximately four years ago, after several days of almost

continuous emotional pain (decidedly different from the periods of monthly depressions noted above), a warm feeling engulfed me from head to toe. There was a tremendous God Presence about me. My immediate family flashed before me, and my heart and soul stirred with a sort of heated passion that lasted only a couple of seconds (I don't know any other way to describe it). At that Moment I felt the love of my family. It was not until that Moment that I had ever truly felt the love of another human being. Mentally I knew that my family loved me; I knew there were others who loved me, but I had never felt it until that Moment! And I literally was in awe of the feeling. I immediately thanked God for I knew that another miracle had been granted me.

About six months later, again coming out of another emotional and painful journey, a similar sensation overtook me. This time the Light was allowing me to feel love for myself for the first time in my life. I knew then that establishing true love for another human being had taken a giant leap. I also realized that I really could not love you without loving me first. Sometimes I wish that I could be more descriptive about these events, particularly when trying to share them with others. I resign myself to the fact, however, that I can describe these happenings as much as it is intended for me to describe them. Now when one of those nonspecific periods of emotional pain engulfs me, first of all, I know that I'm going to get through it, and secondly, I am expecting some type of miracle at the end of it. To date, this has occurred two more times.

* * *

Paul had a brilliant mind. The academic part of school came easy to him from what I observed. Almost no effort was required for him to get by with the grades of an average student. His handwriting was a smooth and unnaturally good for a man as mine reportedly is. Paul was gifted athletically as well, though he never participated in organized sports in school. In fact, Paul never allowed himself to show to any significant degree what he was capable of, academically or athletically. He would run for miles at a time occasionally. I knew without thinking about it much why he chose to run. I am sure that it was with him as it was with me, running from the pain was very soothing to the soul. Paul tended to be quiet and he generally associated with only a few people. Of course, when he discovered alcohol, his abused child began to express himself on a frequent basis.

The tears would come, along with the often repeated statements: "I don't care." "Nobody cares about me, anyway." Time and time again he would say those things – upon reaching a certain level of intoxication.

Paul, too, served for an abbreviated period in the military. Because of the drug use and the many emotional upheavals, he was also discharged before his time. He, like me, had a difficult time with the authority figures. There were several neck and back injuries that occurred while he was drunk or high while he was in the service. Watching Paul go through his military trials and tribulations, I resolved that I would never voluntarily join any branch of the service. That did not turn out to be the case. Somehow Paul got the message that alcohol simply did not agree with him. He stopped drinking; and for seven years he only smoked marijuana and popped an occasional pill. He was able to function socially acceptably following that prescription. He married, divorced, and remarried, producing two daughters, Sharon and Crystal.

After that seven-year period, Paul returned to the bottle. It was in short order that his abused child reappeared as well. Paul called me (in Tennessee) approximately two weeks before his fatal car accident to inform me that he was going to kill himself. He said he felt that his family would be a lot better off with the insurance money from his death than him being alive and there. He was drunk when he called, which was always the case when he thought of suicide and the days of abuse we experienced in New Jersey. Paul acknowledged during that conversation that he had never soberly spoken with anyone else about those times other than me. And he would only talk about them with me when he was intoxicated. I remember not being overly alarmed at his mention of suicide, for

Paul had on several occasions before noted such an intent, but had never followed through.

When the phone call came from North Carolina about Paul's death, I felt immediate sadness, but at the same time, an immediate sense of relief for him.

The autopsy revealed a high concentration of alcohol and Quaaludes. And I knew in my heart that he had intentionally not come out of that curve in his red Grand Prix, in spite of what the official police report stated. Though I had always dreaded attending funerals, I went to his. Looking at him lying in the casket during the funeral, though he was obviously swollen from the accident, I saw that sense of peace about him he had longed for, for 36 years, that sense of peace that had been given to me during my stay at the Samaritan Center in Nashville four years earlier.

I had tried to share that experience with him, but he chose not to hear it.

Paul was now free from his pain, but I was not free from him. I thought of him often; I felt his old pain. Every year around the time of his death (November), I would really begin to hurt for him. I simply was not able to let go of him – in that way. This pattern of grieving would continue for almost six years. Toward the end of October 1994, I got the opportunity to visit a neighboring school system and do a series of drug prevention presentations to junior/middle school students. A part of my narration included a story about a young man named "Paul" who had been abused as a child and ended up turning to drugs as an adolescent, and so on ... sound familiar? I told this story seven times within a two-day period (Thursday and Friday) to seven different audiences.

The following Sunday upon returning home from church with my family, I was heavy-hearted about Paul. I walked past Curtis Jr.'s room on the way to my bedroom to change clothes. I noticed a sheet of notebook paper with some rather large lettered-goldish-yellowish printing lying on top of a stereo speaker that was close to the door and hallway. I immediately stopped out of a sense of curiosity, and entered my son's room and picked up the piece of paper. On the paper were inscribed these words, written in nearly perfect printed capital lettering: "CURTIS, PAUL SAID GOODBYE." Trying hard not to think anything unusual, mystical, spiritual, etc., I went to my son first and asked him about it; he knew nothing (they were not studying Paul in Sunday School). I next gathered Evelyn and Chloe in the hallway outside Curtis Jr.'s room and inquired of them about the note. They too knew nothing but were impressed with the color-scriptive quality of the message. I placed the note back on top of the stereo speaker and went to my bedroom to change.

Soon we had put on leisure clothing and made it to the kitchen for a snack. After eating, I proceeded back to my bedroom, again passing my son's room and noticing the top of the stereo speaker. The note was gone. No one in my family had seen it since I had placed it back on that stereo speaker approximately 30 minutes earlier. It was never seen again. At the Moment of realizing that the note had not been removed by any of my family, that same warm-chested/soul-stirring feeling came over me. At that Moment I felt my releasing the pain-filled grief for Paul. I was free now as I knew he was free and at peace. And I knew that I had been granted still yet another miracle. I have not hurt for him since.

* * *

Late January through mid-February had always brought intense pain and concentrated thoughts about Mom. When that time rolled around in 1995, it was put upon me to call my brother, Larry, and talk about it with him. Larry admitted that he, too, went through something similar every year. Then my sister, Emmie Lee, would acknowledge the same thing as well upon talking to her. Prior to that, none of us had discussed Mom in such a way before. It was also during that conversation with Larry that we said, "I love you" to each other – a first. Never before had we verbalized such feeling to one another. I would call one of Mom's surviving sisters and a cousin of mine, questioning them about her. The consensus was – Mom was a good person, though pretty much her own person, but good nevertheless. I would find out also that she had actually died the day after my youngest brother, Emmanuel, had been born – because of the hypertension/diabetic conditions. The ominous warning of her physician had proven true.

Since we had not made it a habit to acknowledge or celebrate birthdays growing up, I did not know when Emmanuel's birthday was! So, I would call Morven; his birthday was February 5th, meaning Mom had, in fact, died on February 6th. It all began to make sense to me now. Approximately three months earlier I had watched the movie "For The Boys" and had recorded Bette Midler's rendition of the old Beatles hit, "In My Life." The first time I heard the song, I knew it held some special significance for me, even though I did not understand what that significance was. I put the tape of the movie away. About a week and a half prior to the beginning of my inquiries about Mom, I had this tremendous urge to pull the tape out and play the scene where the song was done. And I would replay the scene/song over and over again, getting an unexplainable, soothing feeling from it.

It was Valentine's Day and lunchtime. I had come home from work around noon with flowers and a card for my wife. I don't remember which one of us brought up my Mom, but I remember tears beginning to roll down my face while sitting at the kitchen table. I pulled myself together after a few minutes and returned to work. I got home around 10:00 p.m. from a part-time job that evening. A couple of days earlier I had purchased a CD of the movie sound track and recorded on both sides of a cassette that one song, "In My Life." I would play it at every opportunity: in my car, at the office and at home. Evelyn would grow irritated with the song.

After finishing some measure of my dinner that night, I stepped into my garage to smoke. As soon as both feet hit the garage floor, the song and Mom flashed simultaneously in my mind and, yes, I saw the flash of light again, and everything became clear to me. In the song, it was my Mom talking and apologizing to me and reassuring me that even though she had at one point in her life placed her needs and desires over me, she had truly come to the point before her death of loving me much more than any of those other people and things. Needless to say, that overwhelming sense of relief and release came and I was free. I forgave Mom at that very instant for having left me. The miraculous had occurred yet again.

Today, Mom serves as a reassuring sounding board for me. Between her and the Spirit that I serve, I have a tremendous "team" to call upon in my time of need. With little demons (periods of depression and intermittent self-doubt) still waiting for me to falter, they represent a comforting source for me. I think about sometimes how, during much of my life, primarily from late teens to adulthood, there has nearly always been a surrogate "Mom" provided for me. Generally, the relationships would blossom quickly, with me and that surrogate Mom comfortable with our roles. I think that the several ladies that have filled this capacity for me have been very honored to do so. I was and am grateful for them.

I wish that I could say that such a miracle of forgiveness and resolve has also occurred with my father, but that is not the case. Perhaps I continue to hold on to the anger without any true desire to let go of it. Perhaps I am not ready to handle this particular phenomenon. I tend to think the former is true. Being honest with myself dictates that, even though over the course of years since his death I have been gradually able to let go of a lot of the hate, I have been unwilling to truly forgive him. Knowing that my father assuredly had some assistance in becoming the abusive and insecure person that he was, has helped my anger to ease. There is compassion and understanding for anyone who endures that negative path and evolves into ... But, at the same time, the compassion only goes so far, because all who are victims (with the exception, perhaps, of the truly psychotic) can still choose to be and to do differently. Sure one will falter; one will hurt self and others at some point in time, but one can still choose to expend the necessary time and energy to reach that place of functional peace. And I understand very well that I will be the beneficiary when I get myself to the point of being completely willing to forgive him. And willing is all that I need to become free of the burden. The Spirit will work Its magic at that particular time.

8
Living Human, Living As Myself

> *"(Self) honesty is that quality of character which comes from understanding that Consciousness is the only reality, and that whatever we are, have and do is the outer manifestation of our indwelling nature. Dishonesty is the betrayal of the real self ..."*
>
> — *Science of Mind*

I often find myself in my work as a psychologist and motivational speaker talking to folks using the expression "Everything starts at home." In explaining the statement I generally offer that we can look at home in two different ways: 1) home being that physical structure that we live in, and 2) home meaning within me. Many a wise man has laid claim to the belief that it does not matter what conditions one may have risen from, it is still a self-responsibility how one chooses to respond to stimuli, especially other people. I bring this thought to page because of a need to relate my current state of being. There is no doubt in my mind that the miracles described earlier are very real, very profound and very significant. I truly believe that my life as it was would have continued and perhaps reached a deadening phase had this release not been granted. I believe I would have returned to the indiscriminate and willful use of alcohol and other drugs. Despite having been granted a reasonable measure of happiness over the last twelve years, other demons created from a distorted past continue to create emotional havoc on a far too frequent basis.

As stated earlier, despite what was done to me, I must, as

Living Human, Living As Myself

much as I am able to, choose to react to people, places and things in mentally, emotionally, and spiritually healthy ways. At the same time, I need to be gentle with myself when I fall short of that ideal. After all, I am my own worst critic, tending to be harder on myself than anyone else. Everything starts with me. The road to recovery from extended abuse is both difficult and enlightening at the same time. It is also a journey that most of us so afflicted will struggle with to some degree for a lifetime. This bit of realism I accept, along with the challenge of facilitating (doing my part) the mental part of my healing process. I have no intention of wavering from this constant climb toward consistent emotional, mental and spiritual wholeness.

The AA Community, which has played a major role in my recovery process, is known to speak of character defects and the damaging blows they can and often do deliver to the alcoholic personality. I tend not to like the terminology character defect, however. For one who has already been thoroughly entrenched in most cases with negative self-beliefs and feelings of unworthiness, this concept can play a little too hard on that already pulverized soul. Despite what concept is used or preferred, there are things about the personality and character of every human being that hinders (some more than others) spiritual and emotional development.

* * *

At one point in my life I felt that my total existence was consumed, ruled and dominated by fear. In many respects, fear has been one of my challenging foes; fear of myself, fear of others, fear of expectations, fear of intimacy, fear of rejection, ...fear! I was constantly in such a state of fear (and anxiety) that even when I retreated (which was as often as possible [unless drinking or using]) to total seclusion from others, I still was unable to completely relax or feel a sense of security. I would notice the tension in my arms and hands, especially. No matter how much I would try not to think, my mind would seemingly race non-stop anyway. Prior to the miracles, thought of imminent doom and dread would hit me several times a day, depending on what particular function I found myself engaged in at the time. For a long while, knowing why I was going through such thoughts and reactions appeared not to help much. But over the course of healing time there has been granted to me a significant measure of relief from this malady.

Only when fear of myself began to dissipate did my fear of people and situations begin to decrease also. The tremendous battle waged intra-personally regarding my self-worth has reached legendary proportions. It remains a daily effort, fortified by mediation, prayer, affirmations, telling myself, telling that still partially bruised inner child of mine, I love you, Curtis; I love you. I do this at least seven times in the morning and at various times throughout the course of the day. I choose to interact with the positive spirit of others. These things enable me to move toward garnishing increased feelings of acceptance and love. I must make such an effort for me first. I am convinced now that it is a must that I be so selfishly focused – for as I relate to Curtis, so shall I relate to those around me. Again, everything starts at home. I believe this type of self-concentration to be a must for all human beings if we are to better serve our fellow man. It took me quite a while to understand that this mode of selfishness was of a totally different brand from what the mind generally conceives upon initial notation.

The fear of true intimacy with another human being continues also to be a struggle for me. There exists still a partial wall around me, protecting me from the potential pain, hurt and disappointment of that special someone going away and leaving me. This abandonment can be in the form of death or the ending of a close relationship. I stand guard, still, constantly against this happening to me again. After all, my Mom left me; grandma gave me up to my father knowing that he was not fit to be a parent, and I was seemingly rejected by every young lady whom I wanted during my pre-adolescent and adolescent years. Because of the miracles in my life, that wall has begun to topple, brick by brick, one at a time.

I have often been amazed (and saddened simultaneously) at how much easier it is for me to show affection to an acquaintance or complete stranger, than it is for me to display such affection to one supposedly closest to me. Because I have shown my vulnerability to that one closest to me, that individual has more power to hurt me emotionally than anyone else. It suffices to say that still in my life, it is better for you to be number two or higher than to be my number one. Early on in our marriage, Evelyn would make this statement to me. "You're not capable of loving anyone!" The words would pierce me deeply because I knew how hard I was struggling to overcome. Even though I knew that she was caught up in her own emotional baggage, I would enter therapy shortly after that statement. I knew I needed to take a closer look at me, in spite of anyone else's shortcomings.

I would learn some things about myself (and about Evelyn) during the course of that counseling stint. One of the things that became profoundly clear to me was: "The closer you are to me, the greater chance you have of hurting me emotionally." I think because my wife saw that I was willing to seek professional help, she became more tolerant of me and my inability to show consistent affection. And yes, I am guarded to a great degree still. I pray to God that this will someday cease to be so profound.

* * *

That initial stint with counseling or therapy allowed me to accept the fact that my personality, for good or bad, is different from most folks. At least according to one personality instrument, The Beck Inventory, only approximately 1% of the people in the world have my particular brand of individuality. Since I had always considered myself to be so different from everybody else, that revelation was pleasing to me. These things I agreed with. Remembering the times I had longed to be like, to feel like everyone else, this official revelation felt good, being different felt good. I tend to be an intuitive sort of fellow who learns more judging (definitely not always a positive thing) and I am a natural introvert. I have been blessed to come into myself more, my gift of entertaining (motivating) others has me wanting that huge crowd before me. In fact, when I am in my element, in my entertaining mold, the more people there are before me, the more I like it. And this is certainly a contradiction of sorts. I willingly expend a great deal of psychic, emotional and physical energy in doing what I do.

Choosing to enter therapy I view as a positive thing, a sign of positive mental health. It is not a joke or something to be laughed at, as some lay people frequently tend to make it out to be. Since I am also a Psychologist by gift and educational training, I had little problem acknowledging the need. I would enter therapy a second time about three years later with the lady mentioned in the acknowledg-ment section in the front of this book (R.N., PH.D.) If there ever was an individual designed for therapy and meant to guide and assist others in the healing process, this lady is the one. She would help me make peace with some of those past demons and accept myself for being who and what I am. I felt nurtured, loved, appreciated and accepted. She was a proponent of hug therapy, which I needed, wanted, and looked forward to (she was not a threat). Her insight into my human nature was uncanny and I was rarely able to not be truthful; actually, I wanted to be truthful with her. I understood very well that RN could guide me along the path of healing only as far as she had taken herself. I was impressed with her honesty and willingness to share herself. She had come far. There is no doubt that God sent her into my world to facilitate that particular part of my healing process.

* * *

For all the miracles, for all the healing that I have been blessed to experience, I am still very much an angry individual. As always, the greatest portion of the anger is directed at myself, for …Though I am now able to understand the concept of myself being a fallible human being, my imperfections are still sometimes difficult for me to take. I get angry with myself to an unhealthy degree whenever I have allowed myself to fall back into that role of Junior God and things fail to turn out as I want them to, or I allow people to simply take advantage of me. It is very difficult still for me to completely satisfy myself. It is very rare that I can accept my lack of perfection on a consistent basis. A portion of this is good, because it keeps me striving that much more to improve, to get better, for such a desire can only enable me to move closer to the point of true self-actualization.

I must be careful of the anger reaction toward me. It is a habit that over the course of time has become so ingrained in me, that I will sometimes fail to recognize its presence, until I have taken that anger out on someone. I get angry with myself most often for allowing others to dictate my thoughts and emotions, thereby dictating my actions or my lack of action, as the case may be. I want to be totally and completely in control of my emotions at all times. But the truth I know; the day that I leave this world from a physical plane, I will still be reaching and striving for such an ideal. My quickness to still get upset is indicative of my not having come to accept myself totally and completely, without reservation. As my self-love continues to grow, so does the anger against me dissipate.

There are several ways that let me know I've got a problem with me. Road Rage is one such avenue. I don't have nearly the problem with the way other folks drive when I am relatively happy with myself and the way my life is moving upward. During my raging and venting I am protected to some degree by a two thousand pound plus vehicle as well! How dare one so blatantly disrespect me on the road! The person must be a sick and totally selfish individual. Then again, he or she could be just a mean-spirited racist. Though I do not doubt that some of the inconsiderate actions of others are intentional, the greater numbers are the opposite. But I am so caught up in my own pain, my own disappointment, my own disillusionment, that I oftentimes fail to see those situations clearly and accurately.

The anger on the road has come hard and instantaneous on many occasions. When the dust settles from such instances, I am amazed and embarrassed by my reactions. When I am not in my element, I take the actions of others personally and many of those old feelings, hurts, and pains resurface for that particular Moment. The road rage is something that I can consciously control when I choose to control it. That control comes with more of a struggle at certain times than others, depending on what's going on with me already. I have actually turned my car around on several occasions and chased folks who have dissed me on the road in some way. The anger and the negative emotion were real, but I knew while the chasing was going on that I was only "selling wolf tickets," meaning, I would do nothing even if I managed to catch them. Sometimes I would rationalize that I only wanted to shake the person up a bit by his believing that I could have been one of those people who would have sought vengeance for their indiscretion. Given the distorted nature of some human beings today, I realize I oftentimes put myself at risk of harm with such reactions, whether the diss was intentional or not. I get the feeling that I am not the only one out there displacing or projecting my anger onto others!

    I tend to be more patient, more tolerant, and less angry when I am being those things with me. I want badly at times not to be angry with others, in spite of myself. I want no longer to be angry with God. The truth of the matter is, because I still hold some anger toward myself I probably still do for those other entities. Choosing to get out of myself by focusing or concentrating on doing something positive for someone else has proven to be the most effective avenue I have found to counteract that anger. An unexpected smile or kind word from someone, particularly from a small child, will also get me out of that mode of being, at least for a while. My anger is me and I am my anger. And I know that I must continue to put forth effort, continue to be willing to let the unhealthy part of it go or have it removed.

* * *

    My dreams have always, to some degree, made me aware of what I subconsciously thought about myself, in spite of any conscious fixing of my mind to the contrary. Alcohol and certain other types of drugs served a similar purpose on a frequent basis during those periods of heavy use. Those blackout times when related back to me were definite signs of my true inner thoughts about me (and others).

    Whenever those dreams were prevalent during my night's

sleep, whether I could specifically remember details or not, I was always left with a negative feeling about myself the following morning. The dreams that detail my anxiety most frequently include those where I end up getting lost or separated from everyone else, or I am running late, about ready to miss an important event. It is the feeling of being lost that comes through with more force than any of the others. Looking back at my life, not coming to know who I was for a very long time and feeling abandoned or left behind were very real, very developed parts of me. These days, those particular dreams come less often, and I find myself not getting lost to the same degree; being lost tends to be more of a temporary condition rather than a permanent and hopeless one.

I used to dream a great deal about mean and evil people. In the dreams, the fear of this particular mold of people was genuine. I generally did well in terms of handling most other things that came my way, but the evil people stopped me dead in my tracks and my fear was enormous. No matter how I wanted to force myself to fight these folks, I knew that they had an advantage over me: they could hurt me without guilt or conscience. I would have a difficult time. The evil people, I'm sure, were representatives of my father and others that had hurt me physically, mentally and emotionally to a significant degree.

The one other dream that created fear and anxiety for me revolved around the world coming to an end and Jesus returning to claim those who are worthy, and to disclaim those of us who did not make the cut. For most of my life I have felt unworthy of God's love, and unworthy of love from my fellow human beings (well noted in other areas of this text). Since the several miracles a few years ago, I have not had this dream anymore. There has actually been one I can recall with the heavens opening up, signaling that second coming, and there was no fear.

The relative peace established with God and the perception of Him being loving and kind rather than punishing and uncaring is apparent.

I look forward to having dreams where I show no fear of the evil ones, where I get to exactly where I'm going and getting there exactly when I'm supposed to get there. There are no feelings of being lost and there is an even more positive reaction to the parting of the clouds. That is and will be progress, and that is what life's all about; growing, changing, getting better on both subconscious and conscious levels, in spite of the differences in individual starting points.

* * *

Over the course of my life I have run for miles and miles. Literally, as an athlete, I have experienced the pain and discomfort of conditioning, of pushing my body to its maximum capacity. I have, at the other end of the spectrum, felt an unbelievable natural high when my body has reached in-shape conditioning after a period of regular and consistent training. There has never been a high that matched that special feeling. I felt as if I were walking on air and could run forever without ever tiring. I recall feeling such a thing on two occasions as an athlete.

Metaphorically, I have also run my whole life – from myself. The miracles have afforded me the opportunities to slow down and occasionally, stop the trek ? away from me. I was afraid of me; I was afraid of what I might find if I stopped long enough to look at me. Meeting and accepting oneself is the way of the mentally and emotionally healthy individual. For much of my life I have not been an emotionally healthy individual. I ran from the pains that had already manifested themselves; I ran from the possibility of more pain. I ran; I ran; and I ran some more.

I am extremely grateful for having come to accept as much of me as I have. But honesty and reality dictate that I still have a long way to go before that acceptance is total or complete. When I run from me today it is usually as a slow jog, as compared to the one-time all out sprint. That is growth; that is being willing to change; that is some fear subsiding; that is me allowing the Power of the Spirit to work its magic in my life. The respite (accepting) periods are not quite so far apart any more either. I will even hang around in that respite area a short while longer before commencing my jog again. When I become aware that I have one facet of myself about which I feel good and acknowledge gratitude, soon I become aware there exists yet another entity about myself I have a problem with. And so the struggle continues. Again, I believe it to be a lifelong task.

I long to be able to say I have stopped running completely and fully accept all the dark tenets of my personality, but to do so would be a lie. Given all the stressors that society puts upon me, I grow tired and weary at times. I still occasionally have thoughts to quit, and my little-boy-lost syndrome temporarily reappears. But deep in my heart, I believe that such would not be a fulfillment of my destiny. I truly would have failed. This I cannot do; this I will not do. The mental image I once had of being of the Cro-Magnon man physical features, of being no good to anyone, of being so unGod-like, continues to dissipate. The changes are not coming as quickly as I would like for them to come.

* * *

I was told once by an acquaintance that I have a tendency to voice thoughts out loud that most of us have but are supposed to be keeping to ourselves. Perhaps I have already done too much of this already in this dissertation. I understand also, that those who read this (and other revelations in this book) and who have occasion to be around me may wonder about my ultimate motivations in my interactions with them. Regardless of that possibility, this section must be incorporated.

The mind games I have played with people and continue to play to some degree primarily represent avenues of self-protection and self-gratification. We all play them at various times in our world! I sought and seek protection from being hurt, from being used, from being ridiculed. I engage(d) such behavior to have my way, to get what I want. In certain circles, I have made the statement: "I am a Master Manipulator, Retired." In all of my confusion and inability to accept who I was, I would frequently choose to play the role, in an attempt to use you before you used me. This pattern of being was born out of the persistent experiencing of abuse and pain. This is no justification for my actions or lack of actions, just truth as I see it.

There were times when I cried tears of genuine emotional distress, but during my tenure as an undergraduate student, I realized that I would seek to manipulate people sometimes to make them feel sorry for me. Generally, I would get treated better, folks were less likely to laugh at me, and I would likely get what I wanted. For a period of time during my second year at St. Andrews, certain ones made a special effort to comfort me or to give me the particular attention I sought. While real on one hand, I truly manipulated and unduly schemed on the other. Half the time I could not tell if I were being genuine or if I were not.

As I noted earlier, I generally blacked out when I drank excessively. But there were several times I feigned being in a blackout to avoid facing the consequences of some of my actions. One such incident that continues to stick in my mind: I was driving (unlicensed and drunk) a homeboy's mother's car while we were carousing one night. Earlier in the evening I had done a 360-degree turn by accident, when approaching a stop sign. That should have told us both something. I remember playing it off to him as if I had intended to do it. A short while late, I would run the car into a fence attempting to navigate another curve.

I recall jumping from the car and running home, without saying a word to my homeboy (shades of SW and Wingate College). The next morning when confronted about the accident, I would claim to have no recollection of the incident. Because of my well-known drinking episodes and my propensity for blacking out, my assertion was accepted and I was let off the hook – by others, not necessarily by Me. I was very well aware of what I'd done.

There was a time when the mind games were so much a part of me that I would engage in them without being conscious of what I was doing. In spite of occasional thoughts of suicide, I wanted to survive. Being nice to and respectful of others had only created havoc for me. Playing the mind games has slowed considerably today. I am sure that a good part of that has to do with the miracles and coming to love and accept myself – thus feeling more secure. The need to defend and protect myself so fervently has diminished. What I have noticed is that the more I continue to grow spiritually and emotionally, the less need I have to play the mind games.

I catch myself when I blame others for something that was totally of my own making. At one point, everything that went down in my world was somebody else's fault; thus I played the mind games with myself as well. Of course I did, since everything starts with me. I could not stand the guilt I was continually heaping upon myself. I fought back the most effective way I knew how. My coping skills were certainly lacking. And I still have a ways to go.

* * *

In addition to my continuing dislike for funerals, I am slow to warm to the idea of joyfully celebrating and enjoying the holidays. I believe that the basis of my general lack of enthusiasm for such occasions goes back to the days of old. The fact that I did not celebrate my birthday until age 30 has a lot to do with my not being overly enthusiastic when that time of year rolls around. Most of the time it feels like just another day, even though I am grateful to have made another year. It is mentally difficult for me to imagine why others celebrate the occasion with such a passion, though emotionally, I comprehend it very well. A general sense of sadness, along with the positive thoughts of gratitude, still accompany those times.

While I do not have a problem acknowledging the necessity to pay homage to and remember at a deeper level those historical figures and/or events associated with Christmas, Thanksgiving, Easter, Memorial Day, Mother's Day, Father's Day, birthdays of such individuals as Dr. Martin Luther King, Jr., Presidents Day, etc., I have a major problem with the extreme commercialism attached to them. I allow my disdain for the commercialism to further affect my hesitant disposition to fully engage and enjoy the occasions. It is true that the celebrations of our holidays and traditions have gotten more and more out of focus, but I also must climb down from my high horse long enough to know that there is a side of me that would still have a problem to some degree, even without the presence of commercialism.

The hurt feelings experienced during my childhood and the disappointment that was so prevalent during those times have laid an immovable claim on me at a certain level of my mind-spirit-soul. Because of the healing and maturity I experience today, I will grow into accepting and enjoying those occasions more. But, I cannot see myself reaching the point of turning cartwheels because of them. I believe that the majority of us who suffer from the holiday blues, a.k.a. depression, do so because of our past negative experiences associated with those times and others in general. It is difficult, though not impossible with the right kind of help, to keep from continually revisiting those old emotions that were painful during those particular times. A lot of people have difficulty even recognizing that emotional connections and associations have played a significant role in our current world. Being able to see these probable connections will afford most of us an intrinsic avenue to include mentally reshaping our thoughts to better deal with these times.

* * *

Psychosomatic illness and ailments caused by the mind, nevertheless very real, plagued me for several years after my recovery process began, particularly after I married, acquired a family and settled into the work arena. I would struggle with both worlds. There would be what appeared at the time nearly overwhelming obstacles still to overcome – within me, as I related to and reacted to what was going on around me. The ups and downs of living often appeared more in control than me.

With those things came increased responsibility and more opportunities for me to be emotionally hurt again. There would be everything from sinus infections (one on average of every six to eight weeks); sinus surgeries (three); knee operations (three); kidney stones (twice); headaches (every day for a single year at one point in time); urinary tract infections (an average of two per year); carpel tunnel syndrome; anemia/ulceretic symptomologies; elevated blood pressure, etc. that I would come to believe were partially, if not fully created by my mental, emotional and spiritual states of being. Worry, anxiety and stress all had field days with my person. The persistent headaches even went back to the days at Wingate College, when I would pop aspirins daily to offset the pain. A co-worker who was aware of my many and continuous ailing conditions suggested to me one day at the office that I might like to read William Glasser's *Reality Therapy.*

Her suggestion was made out of genuine concern for me; I knew that.

Before finishing the first chapter of the book, the light came on in my head. And I became aware that many of those physical problems were in fact created from my own internal stressors. I would pretend that I was not afraid when I really was. I would pretend that I liked being in a situation when I really did not like being in that situation. I would pretend that I was happy in my marriage at that time when I really wasn't happy (fear). I would pretend that I was happy with my job when I really wasn't happy. I would pretend that I was pleased with me when I really wasn't. I would pretend that Paul and Mom being gone did not bother me much when their being gone really did bother me – a lot. I would pretend I liked being around certain people when I really did not. I would pretend that the miracles had fixed everything when in fact the miracles had not fixed everything. I would pretend and I would pretend and the emotional and physical ailments/injuries continued to come ? to come in a very real and painful fashion. Once I was able to stop pretending, the illnesses began to decrease and to disappear.

I am convinced that internal stressors, acknowledged and (particularly) unacknowledged, are the number one source of (my) physical ailments. I offer no scientific data or other supportive opinions from those more notable than myself to bolster my claim regarding this issue. In reality, I really do not care whether one chooses to go along with this train of thought or not. Because of the personal experiences related above (and others not related above),

I am sold on the assertion that as my psychological and emotional states go, so goes my physical health.

* * *

Besides my addiction to ETOH and other drugs, I accept the fact that I stand at risk for engaging in other types of addictive behaviors as well. I have an addictive personality, period! This insight has resulted as I have delved deeper and deeper into myself, along The Road Less Traveled. These other addictive possibilities range from women and sex (not synonymous here), to gambling, to music, to something as simple as the compulsive recording of movies and TV specials, to nearly anything. I feel blessed because I have been able to acknowledge this possibility within myself and seek to control it, thereby not hurting others (and myself). Looking back, I can see where there have been times when my behavior has quickly bypassed the habit stage and moved head first into an addictive course of existence.

My conscious lack of bonding with my Mom or another significant female at an early age, and my inability to form positive, long standing bonds with the opposite sex during my adolescent years, and a once general lack of understanding of what love really is, led to the developed notion in me that sex is love. In other words, making love is how you show that you love. It has taken me a long time to come to accept that this has been my basic mode of operating, specifically during my marriage. This idea has led to many hurt and rejected feelings on my part. Seeing through clearer eyes today, I understand that it is the heart that should abound in a true intimate relationship. Having that knowledge has made life much easier.

Sometimes I wish that I was not cursed with this potentially negative and potentially devastating affliction. I wish I was normal. There are times when I grow tired and weary. But I choose to be conscious of my thoughts, thought patterns, and my true motivation for the things that I do to and for myself and others. I must be aware of having any unjust expectations of others. At the same time, I must not crucify myself for being imperfect in my dealings, and in handling specific situations, especially given my true disposition not to intentionally hurt others. Such an affliction is not necessarily all bad, for there are many positive addictions out there that I would (and have) done well to allow them to manifest themselves.

I have a healthy fear of the power of the addictive process; for, truly the strongest ally of addiction is denial. I choose to be aware of this condition more so for me than for others. Understanding that if I choose to do right by me, I will more likely choose to do right by you. I no longer have a need to assist with creating guilt and other demoralizing feelings. Once, that was a more comfortable existence for me, in a very sick way of course. Allowing the dark side of my addictive penchant to dominate my world would do just that. But it is a part of me that I must embrace, that I must accept as being a part of me; it will consume me otherwise. By accepting this, I gain some measure of control. I do not think for a Moment, in all of my 1% uniqueness, that I am one of only a few who has to deal with things of this nature. I am aware that other folks may struggle more in this area that I currently do. My hope is for them to have a degree of sanity restored to their world, as I have to mine.

* * *

The term religion tends to carry a negative connotation for me, while the concept of spirituality is much easier to accept and identify with. I know that such truth has a great deal to do with the negative experiences described in this book. I have never been comfortable worshiping God in church or other public arenas. In the black church, we tend to be more vibrant and expressive. That has been our history and there are aspects of that experience that I truly enjoy. But I am oftentimes uncomfortable in it as well. It is seldom that I react in that vibrant and expressive manner. It is seldom that I will allow myself to wholeheartedly participate in the "Amen, Reverend"; "Go on preach, Reverend." Neither have I been able to consistently comply with directives from the pulpit. It is not that I intentionally want to be contrary, but it is not my basic mode of spiritual expression. None of this is anything personal against Pastor Walter P., for I believe that this man if truly guided by God in his work from the pulpit. I appreciate knowing him also because the man is not afraid to show that he is human.

I have often felt out of place in that environment because of my low key worship manner. I have felt the eyes of judgment from the more expressive folks around me. I have actually heard people sitting behind me during service on occasion whisper to one another, "Watch him; he won't react." At one point I did attempt to worship in the prescribed mode. The concept of putting on a show (that's what it boils down to me) in that special setting makes me cringe. If I am to attend any worship service, first of all, it must be because I truly want to be there; secondly, I must respond/react true to my nature, whether others are impressed or not. I have met others who tend to lean also with the spiritual concept rather than the religious concept. Many of them are the product of an abusive background as well. What does this mean? I really do not know. But, it is true for me that the spirituality concept has a less harsh, less judgmental feeling about it.

I can remember as a child thinking of God as being punishing, vindictive, and unforgiving. I understand now that such a view was largely due to the negative experiences in my world during those times. I recall, after having failed to follow through on one of those "Cross my heart and hope to die" promises to they guys I was playing with at the time, I went home believing that God was going to take my life before the evening was over. We were dropping tree limbs (hanging from a higher limb and dropping down to a lower limb). My fear of falling would not allow me to let go of that higher limb. Not only was I embarrassed by the fact that I was the only one of the group that day that did not accomplish the feat, but now God was going to get me for having lied.

Later that evening, my aunt would notice me acting sadder and more depressed than usual and would ask me what was going on. I shared with her about my broken promise earlier that day and my fear of God getting me because of it. She was able to convince me that no such thing was going to happen and that God understood my fear of the tree limb drops. That conception of God, somewhat softened, would arise time and time again though. No one intentionally taught me to view God in such light; it would be because of the abuse process that such subconscious and topical beliefs had been formed.

Because of the difficulty I have had, coming to have this ongoing positive relationship with God, I consider everything involved in this relationship to be of a spiritual nature. I am not religious; I am spiritual; and my relationship with my Higher Power is a spiritual one. The term religion breathes too much secularism for me; too much of man is wrapped up in the terminology, and I remain uneasy with it. As someone once said, "Religion is made by man seeking to get to heaven; Spirituality is made by God for folks like me who have already been to hell." I am equally convinced that it really does not matter how one chooses to recognize the unique bond with that Omnipotent Entity. It is what's in the heart that matters. Also, I could choose not to believe in or have faith in this God. I could verbalize his nonexistence a hundred and seven times a day, but it would not take away what I intrinsically know, what I innately know to be the truth: "God is real; God does exist." Deep down within one's soul, every human being knows this to be true!

* * *

"Even in my view of you; in my view of us as a world, in my view of things of this world, I will find me as I am; I will find me as I hope to be."

—CDW

* * *

Everybody on the planet knows how precious the family is. Noted therapist, Virginia Satir, has said that more than 97% of the families in this world are dysfunctional to some degree. No disrespect to Ms. Satir's opinion, but I don't believe that there is any family on the planet that can lay claim to being totally free of dysfunction and be absolutely truthful. There is no state of perfection with us individually or collectively.

I am extremely grateful to have been blessed to have an immediate family that when all is said and done, the love that abounds is imminent. Because of knowledge gained from my past experiences with family, I have tried to not have my children experience some of those negative things that were prevalent with me. I, along with my wife, have tempered our discipline (which has included occasional corporal punishment) with love and explanation. By the Grace of God, hopefully we have been able to keep enough of old selves out of the way, to provide healthy guidance and direction for our kids. The times still exist with me in this setting where I am unsure of the reasons for some of my actions or lack of action as the case may be. Being dad and husband has provided immense challenges for me. There are times when these are frightening roles to appropriately, productively, and even willingly fill, for I am truly a work in progress.

I am far more comfortable with giving and receiving emotional and physical love from my children. I do a better job of it with my son, simply because he is the younger. I do not have nearly the problem with expressing myself in such ways with children versus adults. Children are less of a threat to me. The older the child (or person) is, to a certain degree, the more difficulty I have going there. For the most part, my family has done well in accepting me as I am. Without such acceptance, my road to recovery would be much harder. I must, in turn, afford them the same acceptance and allow them to be who they are.

I have always been uncomfortable to some degree with Evelyn's extended family, largely because of the closeness that exists with them. It was something that I had not had the privilege of in such a traditional way. I find it difficult at times to want to hang around and be around for extended periods of time. It is simply not a part of me at this time. Her family's acceptance of me (and all my stuff) has facilitated my intra-personal and interpersonal growth with others tremendously. I have sometimes forgotten that in all their manners of being, they are human beings too. I believe it to have been by the Spirit's will that I became a part of them.

As far as my own extended family goes, I maintain periodic contact with brother Larry and cousin Constance. They basically keep me informed about what's happening with everyone else. The more mature we become, the more we want to see our family growing up in its proper perspective. Besides an occasional phone call, we still don't do the special occasion recognition bit very well. We have, though, grown to appreciate each other more. I think all of us feel fortunate to have been allowed to step from the shadows and be proud of those parts of our family heritage that were good and positive, and, at the same time, openly acknowledge those things that were not so welcome.

The overall decaying family structure in our world today is, indeed, responsible for a lot of the current madness that exists. Our children and young people have suffered and continue to suffer more than any of us. Collectively, we as adults and parents have failed them, this generation of youth in particular. The critical ingredient in my own family and in your family, is the communication of love and unconditional acceptance. It is only then that the struggle to attain a true sense of self is not so great. It is a tall order, but certainly one that we are capable of filling. The question is, how badly do we want to; how much am I willing to look at me and see the changes I need to make within me to better make this scenario become reality. We owe it to our children, to our significant others, and to ourselves to be willing to seek such a path.

* * *

I believe that friends and friendships are essential for the holistic development of any of us. Of course, I am aware that because of the road I had to travel to find me, my acceptance of that friendship status is saturated with caution. I tend to use the terminology, "a friend," very lightly. I am more a proponent of saying acquaintance instead. I take the word to heart. I allow it to bother me sometimes when I hear folks casually applying the term to any and everybody. I understand that this is part of my judgmental and critical mold.

I can use one hand to count the number of true friends I believe I actually have today.

It may or may not be right that I hold myself and others to such a high standard, but it is the place I currently find myself in my continuing journey to self-actualization. I will allow you to call me your friend, but will hesitate when it comes to referring to you as such. A true friend to me is one who knows my dark side, yet loves and accepts me in spite of that awareness. There are very few people in my world where I honestly see that to be the case. If you are really my friend, there will be no mind games between us; there will be no real fear of my losing you because of some unforeseen or unintentional mishap. You may be angry with me for a while. You may be temporarily disappointed in me. But you will forgive me; you will continue to love me.

We human beings are designed to be able to survive on our own if that's the way things come down; if we had to. Being around others; sharing who we are with others; allowing others to share who they are with us, though, is what makes us complete. The Spirit is encapsulated within that process as well. I count myself more than fortunate to be my own best friend right now. I realize also how exceptionally blessed I am to be able to acknowledge that there are as many as four of five individuals that I would categorize as truly being my friend. In this world, we are lucky and out in front of the race to have one human being that fills those shoes.

* * *

I understand very well that the issue of race has haunted man seemingly since the dawn of time, to some degree. It is amazing to me how one human can look at another human, and because of a different heritage, lay claim to be better.

It does not matter how much training one may have received from childhood to adulthood; to perceive yourself as being superior to another human being because of race is pure fallacy. It is demented thinking. It is you choosing to exist in fantasy land. It is you vividly expressing that you have no pure sense of true self. My terminology of "choosing" is intentional, because, regardless of how much training you may have received to the contrary, once you become of age to reason and think for yourself, it becomes impossible for you not to know the truth. You may choose to ignore it.

Because of my struggles with me and learning to express my worth as a human being, I have been more prone to receive help and relief from whomever concerned individual it came from. Love, caring, and concern for me as a person had no color to it. My heart and soul could only see pureness of spirit in action. When the darkness was so prevalent with me, it would not have mattered what color of person or persons delivered it, the pain would have still come. My psyche would have still been shaped and molded as it was. And it is totally natural for human beings to be drawn to places and persons of light and kindness versus places and people of cruelty and negativity.

We cannot reach a state of true self without having knowledge, awareness and acceptance of our heritage. Despite the inherent struggles built into society's system, I am proud to be a Black Man. There is nothing of this world that I would trade for it. It hurts to be looked down upon by others because of my blackness. It hurts that some of my own confused folks have raised their brows at me for associating with the white man too much. It bothers me that all sides show the same ignorance while laying claim to being so different. I am not blind to the overall white man's mentality. I am not blind to the scourge of racism remaining prevalent to some degree until the end of time. The question I must ask myself though is, how can I claim to serve a Spiritual Being who enlightens me with the knowledge that we must treat everybody with love and forgiveness, but yet lay blanket, un-individualized hatred against all white people, or against all Chinese people, and so on. If I do not choose to judge every person on his or her merit, regardless of race or ethnic background, then I am living a lie. I am a lie.

I currently live in an area of the State of Tennessee that has the potential to be one of the most productive and thriving

Metropolitan districts in this country. So far, because of the covert racism that exists here, it has not come anywhere near that potential. There are times when I get the feeling that we are all aware of this, but collectively choose not to change out of our fear of losing a false sense of who we are. The white folks are not willing to give up what they have in terms of status and position (and of course, that unspoken image of being superior) in order to work cohesively together with everyone for the greater good. Black folks are so caught up in the struggle of trying to get theirs, of trying to make the white folks seeing them as equals, that fear of losing what has already been gained, that they do not push the move with any consistency either. Because of the people choosing not to collectively step from this mold of existence, stagnation rules.

Will things ever significantly move in the direction of racial harmony and mutual respect for one another? Yes, it will. Because of the increasing difficulty to survive and maintain in this city, in this country, in this world, we will be forced to let go of race being our primary motivator for our interaction with others. The bottom line, it will come down to a situation of: "the haves versus the have nots." There will be little room at the inn for bigotry. I have no intentions of changing how I view all human beings. I will not allow you to dictate a state of being to me that is so contrary to that Power that I lay claim to serve. About this, I am not wrong: that Power is not wrong. It is many of you who are wrong. And you know this to be the truth.

* * *

Though I claim to be able to work and interact equally well with all ages of people, it is the teenagers that draw me the most. I look at many of them and I see those same pains, doubts, and confusion about self that were a part of me at one time. We adults talk a great deal of rhetoric about our knowing how we as a whole have and are short changing many of our youths, yet we choose not to move beyond ourselves to make that necessary, critical difference with them. It is no wonder that many young people have no fear of dying and have enough anger in their hearts to take another's life without much thought. Their pain is just that great. Their disappointment with themselves, their disappointment with you, their disappointment with me is that great.

Again, collectively, my generation has failed our young miserably up to this point. Please do not take this to mean that individually there are those of us who have in essence done our job with them. I have been credited sometimes with being gullible and "too soft" in my positions of working with the X Generation. Perhaps there is some truth to this. I am of the belief though that such is okay. While they, the young ones, must be held accountable for their own actions, we must teach them compassion – by showing compassion. We must, at the same time, teach them love – by showing them love.

In order for me to be able to teach and educate these X Generationers, I must have the ability to give love, compassion, and forgiveness to me. I truly can not give away what I do not have. To play the role of pretending to care does no good, in fact, it only hardens the heart quicker. They can see through me a mile before I get to them. I must either choose to be real or choose to stay at home. As with some of us (grown-ups), their resilient nature astounds me at times. They truly have more obstacles to overcome to reach a sense of true self – just to survive. I must take the opportunities I am granted to share me with them to heart. It is a privilege, yet at the same time, it is my duty. How can I justify choosing to ignore; how can I justify choosing to tear down rather than build up?

If I am true to me, if I am true to what I say I believe in, I will willingly work my magic with them. I will willingly share the knowledge of self, growth, and survival that has been granted me. They are me and I am them.

* * *

I tend to be a very giving person. It is a part of my original and developed nature to be so. I try very hard not to have expectations of you. The truth of the matter is, though, I do more often than I would like. I often get disappointed when attention or thoughtfulness is not, likewise, returned to me. The martyrdom complex is upon me. Being aware of this condition does allow me some control of it. Having knowledge of myself and from whence I came makes it difficult not to recognize when I am functioning in this mold. I do not like nor do I intend not to seek to work with the Spirit in minimizing its active presence in me.

The martyrdom complex, when at work, negatively affects my relationships with others. If I am so much into wanting from you, then my ability to give of myself to you is stifled. You do not receive my best. I miss out on truly gaining fully from your inner strength and wisdom. I am being blessed with the fortitude today to not crucify myself when I become aware of me being into it. I understand very well that I may never completely overcome this tendency in me because of the depth of my internal struggle at one point. The need to be recognized as being worthy of your efforts, time, and attention remains all too prevalent with me. It is my intent though to continue to strive to totally give of me to you and not have any expectations in return. With no expectations there are no disappointments. With no disappointments in you (or me) I will more value the genuineness in you. Both of us become beneficiaries of something special that was intended to be shared by us. I keep striving.

* * *

I understand that my ongoing problem with authority figures is a direct result of the abusive relationship with my father and the real and perceived mistreatment by others in my world during and after those formative times. I still have a deep-seated disdain for being yelled at or loud talk, as we used to say back in the old neighborhood. Automatic resistance will spring up in me. Whatever your position of authority over me, your tone of voice, whether you ask or demand, will determine whether or not you get my best effort. Even though this perfectionist syndrome exists within as well, it is sometimes relegated to secondary status under such conditions, real or perceived.

In my still sometimes twisted way of thinking, authority figures are representative of the uncaring; you are representatives of the enemy, in a sense. There is an instant resistance to the command to do. In this mold it matters not the voice tone or verbal manner of delivery. My resistance is automatic. The fact that a part of me believes that you only want what you can get out of me makes for my negative reaction. It becomes necessary for quick, internal reprocessing on my part to occur. The current necessity of me having to rely on you for the opportunity to work in order to help support my family makes it easier for this reprocessing to occur. My desire to be in control of me and my reactions, in spite of how something is put to me, motivates me as well. No matter what your "authoritative" role over me is, treat me with respect and dignity; watch how you say to me what you say to me, and you've got a gem of a laborer on your hands.

* * *

In spite of those times, because of my bruised mental and emotional states of being, when music appeared to be more of a curse than a blessing to me, today it serves as an enduring way for me to re-energize, restore my mind and soul in those Moments of just being worn out by the world. I like gospel, rhythm and blues, jazz, easy listening, selective pop, country, and classical. What I listen to and when, has a lot to do with the mood I'm in. Music soothes the savage beast, the majority of the time proves true for me. My road rage tends to be nonexistent when I'm really into the music. I'm not in as big of a hurry to get to where I'm going when the music is working its magic with me.

Music serves as a motivator for me. It is a stress management tool for me. It serves even as a (voice) training mechanism for me. I can get lost or I can be found in its mesmerizing grip. Using it as a part of my meditation regimen, it allows me relatively easy access to my true self. The remaining demons don't stir nearly as much. It allows me to visit with my God and acquire a sense of direction. The resulting inner peace and confidence is indescribable. It is a necessary place for me to travel as I make my way through these times. I love music and it loves me when I allow it to.

9
The Reconnected Psyche: A Final Look

> *There is no doubt today that my path to find me was by design, without such a traveled road I would not be who I am. I believe the ground work continues to be laid for that purpose.*
>
> — CDW

At one time, I thought of the things I endured as being totally negative and self-deprecating. Today, I know that the opposite is true. A line from the Promises section of the AA Big Book notes… "we will not regret the past nor wish to shut the door on it…" As much as possible, I draw strength and determination from my past world. Today I understand that no human being can touch me (mentally and emotionally) unless I give them permission to do so. Admittedly, I continue to give that permission at times.

During the course of this written journey I have hopefully given credit to a number of people for having fostered something positive in me. Though much of my past appeared to be wrought in darkness, it is good and healthy to be able to acknowledge the times that were actually good during that era of my life. I can see even more clearly now, that good. For a while, it was invisible. I think about the many people I know, the many people that I have heard about, who endured "traumas" similar to mine, yet have chosen to blatantly and consistently heap pain onto others. This lets me know that a sense of right and wrong was fostered in me, principally, by Grandma. This also allows me to know that enough positive attention was thrown my way, since I truly could be a totally different person from what I am. It is very easy for one of my training and disposition to just simply say, "the hell with everything and everybody," and set out about the business of intentionally destroying the object(s) of my anger, jealousy, and resentment. My innate God-Spirit, though beaten and trodden down at one pint, was never snuffed out of me. Before the advent of the healing miracles in my life, it was difficult to recognize and acknowledge the love and compassion in my world. It is truly a blessing to now have such an awareness.

    Dr. Susan McMahon, in her book, *The Portable Therapist*, defines self- esteem as "... the placement of yourself in very high regards," She goes on to say: "This means that you not only love yourself but that you act lovingly toward yourself at all times." Assuming that I accept Dr. McMahon's definition of self-esteem (and I do), I still have a ways to go before I can lay claim to acting lovingly toward myself – at all times. Thoughts about my self-esteem have been scattered throughout this volume, both directly and indirectly. The miracle in 1984 at the Samaritan Center leveled the playing field, even pushing me slightly above that 50% mark. My self-esteem has gradually increased since that time. Obviously the road has not been a pothole-free one; no human path is. My honest estimation is that I currently sit at about 72.7 % capacity of my potential for expressing true and consistent self-love. I do not believe that I will ever reach that 100% mark. I believe that the day I leave this earth in physical form, I will be closer to it, striving with a passion to touch that ideal.

    For a while, the nearly constant uplifting of myself, no matter what the audience, was not real. I was faking it until I made it. I knew that; those perceptive folks around me knew that. But I understood then what this process has to be for me. It is about growth; all life is about growth. We all have a choice about whether we move forward or remain stagnant. I choose not to have a choice about the matter. I will continue to move ahead. Those people who have a problem with the matter in which I speak about myself are insecure within themselves. I have been called egocentric, conceited and the like. Early in the beginning of this journey such accusations would bother me from time to time, and I would question myself

The Reconnected Psyche: A Final Look

and my motivation for being me. I no longer question such; I am convinced that in order for me to fulfill my destiny and maximize my potential, I must "stay the course." And this also have I ultimately learned during the course of my expedition: The more I grow in true self-esteem, the more I lose my selfishness and self-centeredness. When I am absorbed in real love for me, the insecurities disappear. I no longer have to be the center of attention. What I would normally seek to get from others I get from myself. And so it is with all of us.

From time to time, I still reflect back on the first 27-28 years of my life, where I was incapable much of that time of having consistent positive esteem toward myself. Sometimes I wonder "what if" things had been different for me and I would have been riding the wave of feeling good about myself all this time; then again that would make me a different person, wouldn't it? I love me, at least 72.7% of the time anyway. The problem comes with me not being able to consistently, genuinely like me for being fallible, for having that dark side about me. Thank you Spirit for not being as demanding (and as slow to forgive) of me as I tend to be.

In my continuing efforts to find and fulfill my destiny (I am actually living a huge piece of it right now), I choose not to accept the standard 9 to 5 existence.

I am not espousing anything being wrong with that mode of operating, for surely many execute their purpose for being on the planet during such a basic course.

But, I do not believe that I will find or complete my purpose by that particular avenue. I have often remarked to individuals, that if I did not have the desire and make the effort to pursue a dream beyond that level, I would surely die inside. And if I die inside, then I will go back to my one time mode of existing in this world. I do not want that again. Included in return to that state of existing would be a probable return to my active chemical abusing status as well, an always frightening thought.

There is a fire that burns deep within me that involves communicating and effecting positive change in other human beings. This is not one of those tangents of old ya'll. I have the ability to make you see you as you really are, not as you may have been told that you are. Only a few of us on the planet have been entrusted with such charge. And I understand very well what a tremendous responsibility this is. If I have such a power to enlighten the soul then I also conversely have the power to darken the soul. I believe I have been thoroughly trained for the mission. It is also true that I will forever be training – it is a lifetime vocation. Though I currently struggle in my endeavors (in terms of the way I want my dream to unfold – sharing me on a broad scale), I maintain belief that "my time (ego), the Spirit's time (total destiny fulfillment)," will come – to a degree. "When I die at the age of 150, I'm going to be so close, I will be able to taste it!

* * *

I offer the following as an attempt to sum up, bring to closure what this expose has been about. The first section provides a list of tenets and manners of being I believe to be prevalent with folks like me, before recovery. The second section deals with the specific recovery process (healing) itself. And finally, we offer opinions and insights about that person we become as a result of the transforming process.

Before recovery, we have:
1) *A poor sense of self, never quite good enough*
2) *Lack of self-love*
3) *Lack of enough self-discipline*
4) *Distorted or irrational thinking for too often*
5) *A susceptibility to drug use and abuse*
6) *Chronic depression*
7) *Lack of trust, self and others*
8) *Emotional instability*
9) *Difficulty forming lasting interpersonal relationships*
10) *A susceptibility to Anxiety Disorder; Panic Disorders*
11) *An unhealthy amount of anger, fear, resentment, loneliness*
12) *A susceptibility to psychomatic illness*

13) Denial tendencies
14) Confusion about Love and Sex
15) Periods of (superficial) non-belief in a Supreme Being
16) Ongoing conscious and subconscious jealousy and envy of others
17) A susceptibility to other addictive behaviors, to include, Obsessive-Compulsive tendencies
18) A tendency to blame others when things go wrong
19) An inordinate degree of fantasizing
20) The presence of "the always searching (love & security) mold
21) The ability to appear cold and uncaring
22) The tendency to overact to the "small things"
23) An excessive amount of selfishness and self-centeredness
24) A huge tendency to be harsh in judgment and criticism of self (and others.)
25) Difficulty asking for help
26) A weakness for suicidal thinking and action
27) A tendency to choose not to see the true motivation of others
28) A tendency to engage the martyrdom complex
29) A tendency to sell out our true selves to receive approval from others
30) The ability to convince self that reality is an illusion
31) The ability to manipulate people and situations – out of a need to survive

A Formula For Healing:

I understand very well that we as individuals travel different paths to get to the point of being able to turn those things that we experienced as having been negative into a constant source of strength and growth for us. This was the path that was destined for me to take. And I offer the following simply as that. If by chance you can find within the following capsuled, personalized formula, or any other thing that I have shared thus far, the motivation and inspiration to begin your journey into finding and accepting yourself, I wish you nothing but success.

1. **Sincere Desire to Heal, to Get Better**
   In spite of the pain that you find yourself in, you must somehow not totally give up on wanting to find an avenue to ease and eventually stop that pain. It is so easy at times to just give up because of the over- whelming presence of that pain. Hold on and know, right down to that last flicker of hope, that it will ease and you will rise above it. It is the essence of true courage to somehow manage to continue the walk, blistered feet and all.

2. **Willingness to Do Something To Help Yourself**
   Being willing to help yourself is critical in this battle to find your true self. The Lord (Supreme Being) will help those who choose to help themselves, no matter how small of a measure the fight may appear to be at any given time.

3. **Prayer and Meditation**
   Belief in a Power Greater Than Yourself is crucial and necessary for true healing to occur. Even if you must pray to a doorknob or a tree because of a temporary state of anger and pseudo-disbelief at the True Power, then do so. Meditate, take steadfast Moments of reflections for yourself and to that designated Supreme Power. As Irene Allemano so beautifully notes: There is no lack, no pain, no sorrow, no separation in Spirit. Choose to go there.

4. **Therapy/Counseling with that "Chosen One"**
   You must avail yourself to that designated individual and be willing to let this person guide you through the maze of your emotional complexity. In actuality, you do not

have to go out and find such a person. When the right time comes, that individual will find you. He or she will ably assist you in plotting your course to true self. And know, that he or she cannot take you anywhere that he or she has not been. That's why the designation: the Chosen One.

5. **Affirmations**
Say strong, powerful, motivating things to yourself, about yourself, every single day. It is essential to offset some of the negatives that have been heaped upon you. The more consistent you are in using affirmations, the more likely you are to come to believe that you are worthy of being on this planet – just like everybody else. Be mindful of the fact that, in general, the human being is largely conditioned by environment and society to engage in negative self-talk nearly constantly. You must choose to do battle with it.

6. **Surrounding Oneself with Positive People**
People with negatively entrenched souls will drain whatever positive energy you may have – if you allow it to happen. Be careful. You don't have to be mean or insensitive, but, it is your right as a human being to love yourself enough to do what is spiritually and emotionally best for you. If those around you are constantly impeding your progress toward

7. **A Constant Vigilance - Faith**
No matter how slow the progress may appear to come, maintain and have an unyielding belief that the necessary healing will happen. You will move to the point of knowing with certainty that your journey to true self is coming ever closer. You have got to maintain long enough for it to happen. And always know that such a journey is forever ongoing. No matter how many psychological and

emotional demons get slain, there will always be other dragons awaiting their turn. That is life. But, in the words of writer and speaker, Mychal Wynn: "No journey is so far that the Spirit cannot lead you .... without the Spirit the smallest obstacle appears insurmountable; with the Spirit you are powerful and unyielding, diligent and determined ...." Maintain the Faith.

After "recovery," which is never fully complete, we acquire:

1) *An uncanny ability to connect with others*
2) *A genuine compassion for others*
3) *An unyielding belief, faith in a Supreme Power*
4) *Self-discipline*
5) *A true sense of self*
6) *A sense of one's purpose for being on the planet*
7) *An ability to motivate, inspire others*
8) *"Presence," wherever you find yourself*
9) *An ability and ease to handle major life stressors*
10) *An ability to overcome challenges and obstacle.*
11) *A heightened intuitiveness*
12) *A penchant for being honest with self and others*
13) *Reflectiveness and introspectiveness*
14) *A willingness to fight for what is right*
15) *An adeptness at one of the "Arts"*
16) *A heightened ability to recognize the truth, no matter the source*
17) *Positiveness and determination*
18) *An ability to work well with others*
19) *The ability to lead or follow*
20) *An ability to adjust to different people, different surroundings*
21) *The ability to put on a "Real Show" on command*
22) *A major dislike for "politics"*
23) *Little or no fear of death*

24) A deep appreciation for positive relationships with others
25) An insistence on avoiding negative people and situations when possible
26) A preference for and ability to appreciate the "simple" things in life
27) An ability to transcend fear consistently
28) An ability to admit character flaws and a willingness to change them
29) An ability to "go to the mountain top" and look over
30) An ability "to leap tall buildings in a single bound" because you truly believe
31) A conviction that a better place awaits you in the after life

* * *

Being honest with myself, I have come to understand, is essential for my survival. It is essential for my continued growth as a human being. I believe the Spirit guides me when I allow It to. Going back to part of my signature noted at the beginning of this book, most of the time I believe I am a tremendously fascinating human being (a part of my retraining and affirming process). All of the time, I believe that my potential for service to my fellows has only minimally been tapped. I hope that when all has been said and done, my journey will have been a great, yet humble one. There is goodness and magic within me and all about me. I have some sense of true self, and it has, indeed, been a journey. I pray for patience in my continuous striving for Spiritual Wholeness.

I leave you with the words of Pierre Teilhard De Chadin, *Patient Trust in Ourselves And the Slow Work of God:*

Above all, trust in the slow work of God. We are, quite naturally, impatient in everything to reach the end without delay. We should like to skip the intermediate stages; We are impatient of being on the way to something unknown, something new, and yet, it is the law of all progress that it is made by passing through some stages of instability, and that it may take a very long time.

And so I think it is with you; your ideas mature gradually. Let them grow; let them shape themselves, without undue haste. Don't try to force them on, as though you could be today what time (that is to say, Grace and Circumstance acting on your own will), will make you tomorrow.

Only God could say what this New Spirit gradually forming within you will be.

Give our Lord the benefit of believing that His hand is leading you. And accept the anxiety of feeling yourself in suspense and incomplete.

Printed in the United States
128839LV00002B/184-210/A